Operation Space Power

The Solution to the Spiritual Energy Crisis

By

GEORGE KING, D.Sc., Th.D.

Printed and Published by
THE AETHERIUS SOCIETY
6202 Afton Place, Hollywood, California 90028-8298, U.S.A.

First Published — August 1987

OPERATION SPACE POWER
THE SOLUTION TO THE SPIRITUAL ENERGY CRISIS

COPYRIGHT OWNED BY
GEORGE KING, D.Sc., Th.D.

Copyright ©1987 by GEORGE KING.

ISBN No. 0-937249-12-2
Library of Congress Catalogue Card No. 87-071807

All rights reserved. No part of this book, *Operation Space Power — The Solution To The Spiritual Energy Crisis,* including all illustrations, may be reproduced or utilized in any form or by any means, electronic or mechanical, including photocopying, recording or by any information storage and retrieval system, without written permission from the Author, George King, D.Sc., Th.D.

Operation Space Power — The Solution To The Spiritual Energy Crisis is printed and published by The Aetherius Society, 6202 Afton Place, Hollywood, California 90028-8298, U.S.A.

Manufactured in the United States of America.

OPERATION SPACE MAGIC
THE SOLUTION TO THE SPIRITUAL ENERGY CRISIS
By George King, D.Sc., Th.D.

By the same Author:

THE NINE FREEDOMS
THE DAY THE GODS CAME
THE TWELVE BLESSINGS
VISIT TO THE LOGOS OF EARTH
OPERATION SPACE MAGIC — THE COSMIC CONNECTION
YOU TOO CAN HEAL
YOU ARE RESPONSIBLE!
THE THREE SAVIOURS ARE HERE!
THE FIVE TEMPLES OF GOD
THE AGE OF AETHERIUS
OPERATION SUNBEAM — GOD'S MAGIC IN ACTION
WISDOM OF THE PLANETS
LIFE ON THE PLANETS
COSMIC VOICE, VOLUME NO. 1
COSMIC VOICE, VOLUME NO. 2
KARMA AND REINCARNATION
BECOME A BUILDER OF THE NEW AGE
THIS IS THE HOUR OF TRUTH
JOIN YOUR SHIP
A COSMIC MESSAGE OF DIVINE OPPORTUNITY
MY CONTACT WITH THE GREAT WHITE BROTHERHOOD
THE FESTIVAL OF "CARRYING THE LIGHT"
DESTRUCTION OF THE TEMPLE OF DEATH and RESCUE IN SPACE
JESUS COMES AGAIN
SPACE CONTACT IN SANTA BARBARA
THE ATOMIC MISSION
A SPECIAL ASSIGNMENT
CONTACT YOUR HIGHER SELF THROUGH YOGA
BOOK OF SACRED PRAYERS
THE PRACTICES OF AETHERIUS
THE FLYING SAUCERS
THE TRUTH ABOUT DYNAMIC PRAYER
IMPORTANCE OF COMMEMORATION AND SPIRITUAL HAPPINESS
A SERIES OF LESSONS ON SPIRITUAL SCIENCE ON CASSETTES.

A price catalogue, with complete list of books and cassettes by the same Author, is available upon request.

All books and cassettes by George King, D.Sc., Th.D., are obtainable from the Publishers, The Aetherius Society, American Headquarters, 6202 Afton Place, Hollywood, California 90028-8298, U.S.A., Tel: (213) 465-9652 or 467-HEAL; or from the European Headquarters of The Aetherius Society at 757 Fulham Road, London SW6 5UU, England, Tel: (01) 736-4187 or 731-1094.

DEDICATION

This book is respectfully dedicated to the Controllers of Satellite No. 3 Who have worked throughout the years to send uplifting, Divine Spiritual Power to all terrestrials on Earth.

CONTENTS

CHAPTER   PAGE

	INTRODUCTION TO THE AUTHOR	9
	INTRODUCTION	13
1	COMMUNICATION WITH SATELLITE NO. 3	15
2	COMMUNICATION WITH MARS SECTOR 8— SPECIAL ADVISOR S2	43
	EPILOGUE	58
	STATISTICAL CHARTS	67
	AUTHOR'S RECOMMENDATIONS	73

ILLUSTRATIONS

ILLUSTRATION

1	THE AUTHOR	8
2	DRAWING OF THE THIRD SATELLITE	45
3	THE SPIRITUAL ENERGY RADIATOR	46
4	THE "KING PRANIC CONCENTRATOR"	47
5	OPERATION BLUEWATER APPARATUS	48
6	OPERATION BLUEWATER	49
7	OPERATION SUNBEAM — ENGLAND	50
8	OPERATION SUNBEAM — U.S.A.	51
9	OPERATION PRAYER POWER	52
10	PRAYER POWER DISCHARGE TO ITALY	53
11	PRAYER POWER DISCHARGE TO U.S.A.	54
12	THE SATURN MISSION — SCOTLAND	55
13	THE SATURN MISSION — U.S.A.	56
14	THE SATURN MISSION — U.S.A.	57

THE AUTHOR

His Eminence Sir George King, Metropolitan Archbishop of The Aetherius Churches; a Western Master of Yoga and an expert in astro-metaphysics, who has devoted his life in service to humanity.

INTRODUCTION TO THE AUTHOR

In the world of metaphysics, or Spiritual sciences if you prefer, there has been a mass of information published dealing with many different aspects of this science. But very little has come to light which compares with the information given in this book.

This mighty step forward into the future of the Spiritual sciences has been brought about by the Author, who has dedicated an important part of his life to, not only this study, but also its application.

Born in Shropshire, England, on January 23rd, 1919, the Author took a natural interest in Religion from an early age, and even in those days, he pursued his interest with a single-minded dedication which few children of the time were able to demonstrate. Years later he was to discover why this fervent interest was inborn in him and where it was to lead him.

After World War II, he turned away from the orthodox type of Religion and practised, with the same single-mindedness, the sciences of Yoga, in which he became very proficient.

In May 1954, he was given the Command by a Master not living on this Earth to: "Prepare yourself, you are to become the voice of Interplanetary Parliament."

He was later to learn that it was because of his single-mindedness and dedication to the Spiritual sciences and mankind that The Cosmic Masters had chosen him for the enormous task ahead.

He was instructed to bring into being The Aetherius Society in order to release some of the information he was about to receive. Despite all odds to the contrary in those early days of the unbelievers, he did found The Aetherius Society in London, England, in 1955.

Later, he was ordered, by The Cosmic Masters, to go to the United States where, in 1960, he incorporated The Aetherius Society as a Religious, scientific, educational organization.

Since the initial Contact, the Author has taken over 600 Transmissions, in a deep, Yogic Samadhic trance condition, from Masters Who are thousands of years ahead of anyone living on this Earth.

He has been through many elevated experiences of a supernormal nature and has learned many things about an ancient yet modern science, which some people call "Radionics." This is the science in which subtle and psychic energies are controlled and directed. The Author performed experiments along these lines, having the burning desire to send Spiritual Energies out to impoverished mankind. He succeeded in bringing about some masterful breakthroughs in this respect.

For the first time, in this modern age on the surface of Earth, prayer, healing and psychic energy could be contained and later directed to any part of the world which was hit by a natural or man-made catastrophe.

He designed Mission after Mission himself, which were later officially accepted by The Cosmic Hierarchy of the Solar System as part of Their overall Plan for the salvation and enlightenment of mankind. He was also given assignment after assignment by The Cosmic Masters for the benefit of mankind.

Some of these feats were published and talked about on radio and television, in newspapers, magazines, periodicals, etc., mainly by others associated with the Author, and the word leaked into high places on Earth.

Honour after honour, including several Knighthoods, were bestowed upon the Author by a King, Princes and Chivalric Orders alike, all of whom highly respected the Author's complete dedication to God, The Cosmic Masters and humanity.

The Author was created and consecrated as an Archbishop and commanded to go forth and found his own Church. Although The Aetherius Society was in operation, he nevertheless was declared as the Metropolitan Archbishop of The Aetherius Society worldwide and uses the working title, correct by ecclesiastical and chivalric law, of — His Eminence Sir George King.

Introduction to the Author

Among the honours, too numerous to detail here, the Author was given the high honour of Freeman of the City of London on June 12th, 1986. Of his many occupations, the authorities chose to inscribe — Author — on the official document. This is particularly significant as he has written many metaphysical books which are known throughout the world.

He was later made a member for life of the Guild of the Freemen of London. He has also been elected an affiliate member of the Royal Institute of Journalists and carries as well, two other well-known press cards.

His Eminence Sir George King has earned many doctorates, mostly of a Religious nature.

From a beginning in Shropshire, a man was born in ordinary surroundings, the son of a village schoolmaster, and from there, because of his work for mankind, gained the respect of others in authority, despite the fact that he was considered to be an unorthodox scientist. Unlike most men, who retire from active duty at the age of 65, His Eminence Sir George King has not done this but is continuing to run and build up The Aetherius Society, which now has incorporation as a Church in several countries.

He also continues to take control of the many Missions which are solely for the benefit of the world and mankind.

Despite the fact that he has written numerous books and published well over 100 educational cassettes, he has not taken any royalties from the sale of these but, instead, has given the profits to The Aetherius Society, his Church, to enable this very active organization to continue with spreading the Teachings and Work of The Cosmic Masters.

All material manifestation is a result of the application of Divine Mind which created multitudinous energy fields in which particles of matter are held in continuous motion.

There is only one energy crisis in the world today — that is, the spiritual energy crisis. If this is put right within the hearts and minds of mankind, then no other man-made shortages can exist.

INTRODUCTION

This book, *Operation Space Power — The Solution To The Spiritual Energy Crisis,* is a report which shows the respect given to the Author by The Cosmic Masters. It is also a true demonstration of the devotion to duty displayed by certain Members of The Aetherius Society who, without complaint, have often worked until the early hours of the morning, for over 30 years, to operate the Spiritual Energy Radiators in cooperation with Satellite No. 3 and thereby gave to the world a legacy never before offered.

Although this book is only a small one, it describes a feat of such magnitude as to be world-shattering in its implications!

The Author, a Yogic Master of vast experience in astrometaphysical matters, has gone out of his way to convey the essence of the Space Communication herein, even to the extent of occasionally seeming to be repetitive, so that he could make sure that all the information delivered by the Cosmic Master from Satellite No. 3 could be given in an understandable way to you, the reader.

That the Author possesses an unusual compassion for mankind is proved by the very carefully thought-out line of questioning which he instituted. This is proved to you by the leniency which was demonstrated by the Cosmic Controller from Satellite No. 3.

In fact, the priceless Spiritual gifts given to the world throughout the past and into the future, as described in this book, **are a means to solve the greatest energy crisis on Earth today, namely, the Spiritual Energy Crisis!**

If mankind were to put that right, then he would enjoy progressive peace, scientific exploration and would want for little else.

The Author has stated publicly many times throughout the years that: **"There is no science without Religion, and there is no Religion without science."**

This fact has dawned gradually on many New Age authors of the present day and it illustrates a trend in the right direction — in fact, the only safe direction!

The Author strongly recommends all keen students to **study this book very carefully,** not just scan through it in a cursory manner, because if you do, you will miss the very essence of the psychological line of questioning and the astounding answers given.

Also, all New Age students are strongly advised to read the material recommended at the end of the book as this New Age material will give you a deep, lasting understanding of, not only the salvation of mankind, but also how **you** can prepare **yourself** to lay the strong foundations for the glorious bright New Age which **you** have to build on this Planet.

Special Note:

So that the reader may understand the separate dates given in this book, the following should be remembered:

On July 8th, 1964, The Cosmic Masters, Who comprise The Spiritual Hierarchy of the Solar System, performed the most advanced astro-metaphysical Operation which had ever previously been reported to mankind — **The Primary Initiation Of Earth.** The Author was privileged to be the only channel through whom the report of this stupendous event was given to mankind and this was subsequently published in his unique book, *The Day The Gods Came.* In recognition of The Primary Initiation Of Earth, the Higher Realms and The Great White Brotherhood altered Their calendars and regarded July 8th, 1964, as Earthyear 1, Earthday 1, and continued from there.

COMMUNICATION WITH SATELLITE NO. 3

This is Santa Barbara, May 22nd, 1987 (Earthyear 23.319), time approximately 10:00 a.m.

I have in front of me some data regarding the Operations of Satellite No. 3 around Terra during what have been officially termed as "Magnetization Periods." The name was later altered, by the Society, and given the name of "Spiritual Pushes." This term was derived from the fact that whenever Satellite No. 3 is in orbit of this Planet, all Spiritual and unselfish activities are enhanced 3,000 times. This information was stated by the Cosmic Master Aetherius in a Transmission delivered through the Author on January 7th, 1956, in London, England. (Note 1.)

The first public announcement of the Operation of Satellite No. 3 was made on May 28th, 1955, and up to May 23rd, 1987 (Earthyear 23.320), this floating Temple of Light has been operating on and off around this Earth for approximately 4,171 days. (Note 2.)

According to information, later received, the Controllers of Satellite No. 3 discharged Spiritual Energies of different frequencies to Levels Plus 4 to Minus 4 (the lower astral realms) from between 130,000,000 (one hundred and thirty million) Prayer Hours to 194,000,000 (one hundred and ninety-four million) Prayer Hours. At the same time, during these Spiritual Pushes, units of Spiritual Energy were discharged to Levels 5 and 6, between 54,223,000,000 (fifty-four thousand, two hundred and twenty-three million) units to 72,922,500,000 (seventy-two thousand, nine hundred and twenty-two million, five hundred thousand) units. A portion of this Spiritual Energy — and we do not know how much — was unused by the inhabitants of these realms and the unused surplus Spiritual Energy was recalled so as to avoid leaving a "resonance factor" in any area. (Note 3.)

However, at this time, having made previous arrangements to communicate with Satellite No. 3, I only asked questions regarding the Spiritual Energies which had been put through our **own Spiritual Energy Radiators.** We call this Cosmic Mission **Operation Space Power.**

On April 22nd, 1958, in a Transmission from the Master Aetherius, we were given information in London on how to build a radionic apparatus. After we had built this apparatus, I suggested that we electrically and radionically tie it in with two other pieces of apparatus which I had previously invented. This apparatus was lovingly called "Gertie and Gertina" by my operators.

On November 18th, 1959, we started cooperation with the Magnetization Periods of Satellite No. 3 and ceased this cooperation with this machine after 1,650 days, on June 6th, 1971 (Earthyear 7.334).

In the meantime, I had set up a Headquarters in the United States and was asked to invent some equipment for a Cosmic Mission termed **Operation Bluewater.** I invented this equipment and it was built on the premises by the then available Staff Members. This equipment was used successfully during **Operation Bluewater,** which was performed off the coast of Southern California over a Psychic Centre of the Planet Terra. (Note 4.) Later, although this apparatus was not originally intended for the purpose, we were asked to cooperate with Satellite No. 3 with it during a Spiritual Push, which we did, starting on March 15th, 1965 (Earthyear 1.251). After 598 days, we ceased cooperating with this apparatus after a Spiritual Push, on October 9th, 1969 (Earthyear 6.94).

One of my reasons for setting up a "Question and Answer" session with Satellite No. 3 was to find out the amount of Spiritual Energy radiated through these machines. Although we kept logs on their use, we had little or no idea of the amount of Spiritual Energy which was sent out to the world and whether all of this Spiritual Energy was used or some of it was recalled.

I also wished to verify the **use** of the Spiritual Energies which had been sent through our own Spiritual Energy Radiators by Satellite No. 3.

During this "Question and Answer" session, I recorded all

questions on a dictaphone and repeated the answers, which were given to me by a Controller from Satellite No. 3, so that I did not have to commit these facts to memory; and even re-checked the information with the Cosmic Master during and at the end of the quite long communication session.

It should be mentioned, at this stage, that just recently, it has become more difficult to communicate with Satellite No. 3 through telepathy because, since the Satellite has been in orbit, more and more publicity has been made about this Space Station, including media broadcasts in England of actual Religious Services of cooperation with Them. Books such as *The Nine Freedoms* and *The Day The Gods Came* have also publicized the workings of Satellite No. 3, as have many other magazines and newspapers throughout the world. Millions of people now know a little more about Satellite No. 3 and its frequent Spiritual action around this Earth. Although some of these people will never think of joining The Aetherius Society, which originally gave them the information, apparently many of them have prayed, individually and sometimes collectively, for help, mostly of a personal nature, from the Satellite.

Now, although Satellite No. 3 is protected by powerful force screens, They do occasionally have to shut part of these down for outside analysis purposes. I think the intelligent reader can imagine what a mass of jumbled requests, most for the wrong, selfish motives, have reached the Satellite. Furthermore, terrestrial publicity on the actions of the Satellite — **which the Controllers did not object to** — would also make the Satellite better known, even in the lowest realms, where evil magicians, **more versed in metaphysical matters than most people on Earth,** could see a way to enhance their power for their own nefarious reasons — or at least, thought they could!

So, the Satellite introduced a coding system. No communication, just recently, is answered from Satellite No. 3 without the use of this strictly secret coding system; and besides that, the telepath must pass through a **mental imprint** which cannot be faked. In that way, Satellite No. 3 protects itself from a mass of extraneous requests, which cannot be met anyway because of the Karmic pattern of mankind.

At this particular time, I had previously made the arrangements mentioned and, having communicated with Satellite No. 3 on and off throughout the years, had been given the mental coding system; and the mental imprint of my telepathic transmissions to the Satellite was duly logged in such a way that, under no conditions could it be faked by anybody.

In Los Angeles 21 years ago, I invented a piece of apparatus called a "Spiritual Energy Radiator" for use in a Cosmic Mission called **Operation Sunbeam.** (Note 5.) This was used in **Operation Sunbeam** successfully for approximately 34 Phases, until I later improved on the modus operandi of this Mission. (Note 6.)

I was then asked by Satellite No. 3 if this Spiritual Energy Radiator would cooperate with the Magnetization Periods throughout the year, and on March 1st, 1969 (Earthyear 5.237), we started this cooperation, for a minimum of three hours per day.

Up to the present time, we have discharged through the Los Angeles Spiritual Energy Radiator, approximately 14,597,730 (fourteen million, five hundred and ninety-seven thousand, seven hundred and thirty) Prayer Hours of Spiritual Energy!

Later, in 1971, a duplicate of the original apparatus which was already in operation in Los Angeles, was built in America and shipped to England and that machine started cooperation with the Satellite on June 7th, 1971 (Earthyear 7.335).

Already, approximately 12,484,800 (twelve million, four hundred and eighty-four thousand, eight hundred) Prayer Hours of Spiritual Energy have been radiated through the London Spiritual Energy Radiator!

In one Operation performed directly from Satellite No. 3, The Cosmic Masters stated that the following frequencies of Spiritual Energies were actually sent out to different Levels of life connected to the Planet Earth:

Level — Minus 4:	Classed as Category D/E
Level — Minus 3:	Classed as Category C/D
Level — Minus 2:	Classed as Category B/C
Level — Minus 1:	Classed as Category B
Level — 1: *(Physical Level)*	Classed as Category A to A+
Level — 2:	Classed as Category A+
Level — 3:	Classed as Category A+/AA+
Level — 4:	Classed as Category AA+ or above

It depends on the result which is due to be brought about as to the frequency of the Spiritual Energy which is radiated through the apparatus.

Never content to rest on my laurels and bathe in the light of past glory, I invented, in the meantime, another Mission, called **Operation Prayer Power,** in which Batteries could be Charged with Spiritual Energy by our Members, then held for emergencies, such as earthquakes, typhoons, disease waves, etc. (Note 7.) The same Spiritual Energy Radiators used in the cooperation with Satellite No. 3 for the radiation of Their Spiritual Energies, can also be used to discharge the Prayer Energy from these Batteries, put in by our own Members.

To date, we have discharged 95,955 (ninety-five thousand, nine hundred and fifty-five) Prayer Hours, some of which have been used in catastrophe areas.

This figure also includes the Prayer Hours we release every week from our **Operation Prayer Power** Batteries during the orbit of Satellite No. 3 during a Spiritual Push, which Spiritual Energy is also used and because of its "terrestrial" frequency, has been very valuable to mankind. (Note 8.)

A Prayer Hour is the amount of Prayer Energy an individual can transmit in one hour of continuous Prayer. As all individuals differ, so would the frequency of the energy radiated also differ. However, we have evolved a system whereby we can estimate the frequency of energy radiated by a fully trained prayer.

The average, good dynamic prayer in **Operation Prayer Power,** for example, puts out Category A+ Prayer Energy, which is very valuable and a very potent Healing Power. We do not allow our standards to fall below Category A. If a person in the Prayer Team falls below Category A, then we put them off the Prayer Team for further practise. We are very strict about this because all prayers are timed to the second and they are assessed by at least one or two assessors as to the frequency of Prayer Energy they put out in these Categories. (Note 9.)

Therefore, since the cooperation with a Spiritual Energy Radiator on March 1st, 1969 (Earthyear 5.237), to date, we have radiated to the world an amazing 27,082,530 (twenty-seven million, eighty-two thousand, five hundred and thirty) Prayer Hours; or 3,091.6 Prayer Years; or 30.91 Prayer Centuries, through our Spiritual Energy Radiators, excluding the Operation Prayer Power hours and any cooperation previous to these dates.

It was to find out further information about the effectiveness of this Spiritual Energy that I opened communication with Satellite No. 3 on May 22nd, 1987 (Earthyear 23.319), knowing that it was to leave orbit at midnight Greenwich Mean Time on May 23rd, 1987 (Earthyear 23.320).

Some amazing facts came to light!

This total of 27,082,530 (twenty-seven million, eighty-two thousand, five hundred and thirty) Prayer Hours, excluding the 95,955 (ninety-five thousand, nine hundred and fifty-five) Prayer Hours released from the **Operation Prayer Power** Batteries, was based on a calculation given by Mars Sector 8—Special Advisor S2 on October 18th, 1978 (Earthyear 15.103), Who stated that each of our Spiritual Energy Radiators, activated at definite times requested by Satellite No. 3, released 2,040 (two thousand and forty) Prayer Hours of Spiritual Energy per hour of machine operation.

This gigantic feat could not have been performed without the cooperation of Satellite No. 3; neither could it have been performed, according to Satellite No. 3 Controllers, without our cooperation by having these machines available to anchor this Spiritual Energy on the Planet. **I suggest the reader studies all** our literature on world Karma! (Note 10.)

I received a reply to my coded identification at approximately 10:15 a.m. in my office in Santa Barbara on May 22nd, 1987 (Earthyear 23.319).

The first question I asked was this:

Question: "Thank You for Your indulgence by opening up this line of communication.

"I will address You as 'Satellite No. 3' if You do not mind, because other people may hear this tape.

"During some Missions of late — and it has only happened just recently, as You know, especially during **The Saturn Mission** — the Spiritual Energy Radiators have been activated in cooperation with four Phases of the Mission. (Note 11.)

"When **The Saturn Mission** took place in England, the London Spiritual Energy Radiator was freed from encumbrance and special runs were made during the actual **Saturn Mission** itself on the London apparatus.

"Likewise, special runs were made by the American Spiritual Energy Radiator when Phases of **The Saturn Mission** were performed over a Psychic Centre in the United States. (Note 12.)

"The total special runs on both of these machines amounted to 148¾ hours of running time, during which 303,450 (three hundred and three thousand, four hundred and fifty) Prayer Hours of Spiritual Energy were discharged.

"The question I wish to ask is: Was all this Energy used? By whom? And if not, was the unused Spiritual Energy recalled? Would You please answer that if not classified information?"

The reader should appreciate the fact that I re-checked all important answers from the Controller from Satellite No. 3, Who allowed me the great privilege of this interview, so as to make doubly sure that I fully understood the answers which were given and was able to explain them in simple, straightforward English in order that the meaning could be fully understood.

Answer: "Some of the extra Spiritual Energy radiated was used as a supplement to the Spiritual Energy released during **The Saturn Mission** and this was manipulated in such a way as to be of the most use. However, as not all that Spiritual Energy was used by the manipulators involved, we had the ability to recall the surplus Spiritual Energy because when we transmitted that Spiritual Energy, we incorporated a certain frequency into it which would answer to recall."

I repeated the answer in my own language on the dictaphone and asked:

"Do I understand that correctly?"

On receiving an affirmative reply, I thanked Them and proceeded:

Question: "We also have another figure here, which is not an estimation and will be correct.

"From 1973 to date, 95,955 (ninety-five thousand, nine hundred and fifty-five) Prayer Hours were sent through the Spiritual Energy Radiators during special manipulations to help in disaster areas. This figure also includes the Prayer Hours which we radiated every week during a Spiritual Push.

"Was all that Spiritual Energy used?"

Answer: "All that particular Spiritual Energy was used — not necessarily at the time, but sometimes at a later date. The surplus was mainly manipulated by Agencies in Levels 4 and 5, and of course, The Adepts.

"Levels 4 and 5 radiated Their own helpful Spiritual Energies as well, to supplement your release. You know that what you call The Great White Brotherhood, also sent extra Healing Energies into these disaster areas."

Question: "Yes, I understand that this tremendous amount of Prayer Energy was used, but not at the particular time it was radiated. It was probably put into the aura of Terra and then was used later.

"Was it all used by people on the physical plane? Or was some of it used by people on, shall we say, different planes, such as the lower astral realms?"

Answer: "A very small portion of it was used by life forms on the lower astral planes."

Question: "Can You give me that portion in percentage?"

Answer: "Possibly about 10 percent was used by life forms on the lower astral planes."

Question: "But 90 percent was used, then, directly by people on this realm, especially during the manipulations which were pinpointed to the target areas, namely, disasters, and were manipulated by The Adepts into those areas?

"The unused surplus Spiritual Energy was then absorbed into the auric belt of Earth over those areas, so that it could be used gradually as the time went on?

"Do I understand that correctly?"

Answer: "You partially understand that correctly."

Question: "How did You stop that Spiritual Energy from pervading the whole terrestrial aura?

"Supposing we sent Spiritual Energy to a place which had been damaged by an earthquake — that would only represent a small part of the aura of Terra. Therefore, do I understand that The Adepts were able to confine that Spiritual Energy to that particular target area?"

Answer: "Yes."

Question: "How were They able to do this?"

Answer: "Because the Spiritual Energy itself was actually absorbed into matter in the particular target area."

Question: "Vegetable matter?"

Answer: "Yes, most of it was confined to vegetable matter for further natural release."

Question: "And that which was not, was confined to what we might call 'humanoid matter,' for want of a better term?"

Answer: "Yes."

Question: "It would appear to me that some people in those stricken areas used the Spiritual Energy very effectively indeed. In fact, there were amazing rescues made, which could not have been accomplished unless the rescuers were reinforced with powerful Spiritual Forces.

"Do I understand that correctly?"

Answer: "Yes, you do."

I was further informed that none of the Spiritual Energy released from **Operation Prayer Power** Batteries and The Great White Brotherhood to these disaster areas, was wasted. If an excess of Spiritual Energy was radiated at any one time which created a "resonance factor," this was balanced by absorption into vegetable matter in that area, to be naturally radiated at a slightly later date. This unused Prayer Energy would thus bring about a natural balance and improvement to the stricken areas.

A modern Spiritual Miracle in action!

I was further informed that Satellite No. 3, although They did not appear to cooperate in these respective releases, were able to make overall calculations of the amount of Spiritual Energy sent out and used, even though They were not in terrestrial orbit at the time of our release. They did this through instrumentation which was lodged at Central Control, a part of which is known to us under the code name of Mars Sector 8—Special Advisor S2.

Readers of *Cosmic Voice* will remember that it was Special Advisor S2 Who originally gave us the timing sequence for **Operation Prayer Power.** Before we received this information we did not know how much Prayer Power Energy was in each respective Battery. (Note 13.)

Readers of *Cosmic Voice* will also remember that some of our Batteries, especially in London, because of their higher attendance to **Operation Prayer Power** sessions than we have in America, were becoming near the full mark and The Adepts were asked to take some of the Prayer Energy from these Batteries and hold it for us. This amounted, in the beginning, to 2,264 Prayer Hours of Prayer Energy. This was a big help to us because it was later possible to send out Prayer Power Energy without activating the Spiritual Energy Radiators. In other words, I could have done this from a remote hotel room somewhere, as I am able to retain telepathic communication with The Adepts and The Great White Brotherhood at the same time, for quite long periods — a feat which is above the capabilities of even an expert psychic!

I was further informed that, in the absence of Satellite No. 3, Central Control, Mars Sector 8, would have overall control of any Spiritual Energy we sent out in **Operation Prayer Power,** although They would not Themselves be **allowed** to interfere by supplementing the amount of Spiritual Energy.

There were odd times during some of these manipulations that a "resonance factor" was created in a certain area by our transmission, which was too powerful for absorption at that time. (Note 14.) That "resonance factor" was completely balanced, possibly by Central Control, so that the best possible use could be made of that priceless Prayer Power by all people concerned, such as rescue workers, people who donated to the cause of earthquake victims, and transport workers who flew in large quantities of medical supplies, fresh water, food and clothes to the homeless. All of these people had available to them powerful Spiritual Energies to absorb, **at their free will,** if they wished to use them. There is no doubt that many of them did so because of the wonderful way in which they worked. Many of the victims had what is termed by the media as "miraculous escapes" during some of these massive disasters. (Note 15.)

I was further informed that only in cases of the most dire national emergency would Central Control be allowed to intervene. I gently informed the Communicator from Satellite No. 3 that I had worked that one out for myself!

Question: "Now, continuing from there, we still have massive figures relating to Spiritual Energy which has been sent through both Spiritual Energy Radiators. This Spiritual Energy, together with the Prayer Energy released during **Operation Prayer Power,** amounts to 27,178,485 (twenty-seven million, one hundred and seventy-eight thousand, four hundred and eighty-five) Prayer Hours — or, for emphasis for my readers, 3,102.5 Prayer Years, or 31.02 Prayer Centuries.

"Now, we have already been informed that some of this Spiritual Energy has been used for the purposes intended, namely, the 95,955 (ninety-five thousand, nine hundred and fifty-five) Prayer Hours released from **Operation Prayer Power** Batteries, some of which was pinpointed to exact target areas and some of which was released during sessions we hold on both machines every week during a Spiritual Push.

"So, leaving that apart, this still leaves us with the release in **Operation Space Power amounting to 27,082,530 (twenty-seven million, eighty-two thousand, five hundred and thirty) Prayer Hours — or, to better illustrate it to my readers, 3,091.6 Prayer Years, or 30.91 Prayer Centuries.**

"Now, even assuming that we have made minor mistakes in our calculations — and these are approximate figures — was all this Spiritual Energy used in the total terrestrial manipulations? If it was not, then I assume that the surplus Spiritual Energy was later recalled so as to avoid the build up of a 'resonance factor' in any area of Earth?

"Is this correct?"

Answer: "That is correct. Not all of the Spiritual Energy radiated in **Operation Space Power,** as you call it, was used and some of it was recalled."

At this juncture, I asked for time to review the proceedings. So I turned back the tape on the dictaphone and let the Communicators from Satellite No. 3 listen again to the questions I had asked, but mainly to the answers which They had given to me. They kindly allowed me to do this, proving, to me especially, that They are indeed not only great Scientists, but well-mannered, cultured, diplomatic Gentlemen into the bargain.

Then, after the review period, I immediately resumed communications again.

Question: "Satellite No. 3, thank You for Your permission to review the material already at hand.

"Some of the Spiritual Energy, then, which was sent through our Spiritual Energy Radiators and during Missions and so on, was recalled because it could not be used at that particular time. In other words, in my terminology, there was a 'resonance factor' which had to be balanced.

"Is that correct?"

Answer: "That is correct."

Question: "Now, where was this surplus Spiritual Energy recalled to? Assuming that it was not used and it had a recall frequency incorporated in it, where did it go back to?"

Answer: "Apart from the **Operation Prayer Power** hours, this surplus Spiritual Energy was recalled to Satellite No. 3 and then later transferred to Mars Sector 8—Central Control.

"The Spiritual Energy recalled, goes down as an all-time 'credit' to you and The Aetherius Society."

Question: "Thank You very much, we are deeply honoured by this action.

"Can You give me a percentage of what is left in what I would term our 'Energy Credit Account'?

"Assuming our calculations are correct. If, however, they are not correct, we could review them and correct them, but a percentage then would be an accurate figure of what may be left."

Answer: "This would be a very complex calculation because of terrestrial weaknesses and the fact that other power radiations were taking place from Satellite No. 3 **at the same time as your Operation Space Power. So, to divide up the different aspects of Spiritual Energy in an exact percentage group would be very complex.**"

Question: "I understand a little about the complexity posed by the answer to this question but some answer would be very valuable to us, especially if we have the 'Energy Credit' You mentioned.

"As a small illustration: The **Operation Prayer Power** Batteries in England were becoming quite full of Prayer Energy at one time and we asked The Adepts to take off a certain number of Prayer Hours, which They did, and They still hold a percentage of this original number of Prayer Hours in 'credit' for us. This is extremely valuable because if there is an earthquake or other natural disaster, we are not forced to run the Spiritual Energy Radiators because we can draw on this 'credit.'

"According to our calculations, the Prayer Energy held by The Adepts as of Thursday, April 30th, 1987 (Earthyear 23.297), was 1,157 Prayer Hours, with a discharge time of 103 minutes. Should another disaster occur, we can draw on that 'credit' without having to operate our Spiritual Energy Radiators at the same time.

"If, for instance, I was located in a remote area without access to either Spiritual Energy Radiator, the Prayer Power Energy could be manipulated by The Adepts, or some of Them, in a free manner, without the limitations imposed by the geographical position of the Spiritual Energy Radiators.

"If one or more Spiritual Energy Radiator is used, I have to control the time of Operation, to a minute, and make sure The Adepts are able to tune into this transmission beam, and then They physically take it to the stricken area where it can be personally pinpointed to rescue workers, who need a powerful Spiritual Force to help them, or for Healing of victims.

"This surplus held by The Adepts leaves me much freer to operate from **any part of the world at any time,** providing The Adepts are able to cooperate with that time.

"As some of the Spiritual Energy radiated through our Spiritual Energy Radiators has been recalled to Mars Sector 8, would it be possible for Mars Sector 8 to operate in a similar fashion to that of The Adepts?"

Answer: "We agree entirely with what you state and can now see why you are asking this question."

Question: "There is a definite flaw in our calculations. Previous to the design and manufacture of the two Spiritual Energy Radiators discussed, we did run other Spiritual Energy Radiators in cooperation with Satellite No. 3. In London, one ran from 1959 and ceased operation on June 6th, 1971 (Earthyear 7.334). The total running time, in cooperation with Satellite No. 3 orbit, was 1,650 days. No release is included in our present calculations because we did not know how much Spiritual Energy was actually put through that particular machine.

"Neither do we know the amount of Spiritual Energy used in **Operation Bluewater** and later, through the ex-**Operation Bluewater** machine, which stopped cooperation with Satellite No. 3 on October 9th, 1969 (Earthyear 6.94), with a total running time of 598 days during the orbit of Satellite No. 3.

"As You know — and to repeat for my readers — the new Spiritual Energy Radiator in Los Angeles started cooperation with You on March 1st, 1969 (Earthyear 5.237), and the London machine started on June 7th, 1971 (Earthyear 7.335). Everything prior to March 1st, 1969 (Earthyear 5.237), cannot be calculated because we did not know how much Spiritual Energy was running through the old machines; although we still kept exact logs of the operating times, up to the time the new Los Angeles Spiritual Energy Radiator started, and then later, when the new London Spiritual Energy Radiator started cooperation with You.

"So, there are some facts which we are sure of when it comes to **Operation Prayer Power** releases and other releases from Satellite No. 3 through the two latest machines; but we are still very much in the dark as to what happened in the early days.

"I realize this is a complex calculation but can it be done? And if so, how long would I have to wait for the answer?"

Answer: "This can be done."

Question: "Thank You very much. How You are going to perform such a task I do not know — it is an absolute miracle to me!

"It would appear to me that You will possibly need some time to divide the two aspects of Spiritual Energy; one radiated some years ago through our old apparatus, which was also undoubtedly mixed up with the normal Operation of Satellite No. 3 transmissions. In other words, I understand that You did not stop terrestrial Operations of Satellite No. 3 when You sent any extra Spiritual Energy through either the old or the more modern machines. So, apart from normal frequency adjustments, it is probably very difficult to divide off the two forms of Spiritual Energy, especially that sent out in the early days.

"I understand that Satellite No. 3 broadcasts different frequencies of Spiritual Energy, such as those acceptable to Levels 4, 5 and 6, and those acceptable to lower Levels, such as the physical plane and beneath. (Note 16.)

"Therefore, does not the whole process of calculation, recall, etc., seem to be a highly complex problem in astro-metaphysics?"

Answer: "We make an allowance from our normal Operation for the Spiritual Energies sent through your machines, and the fact that you are able to broadcast some of this Spiritual Energy also allows us to broadcast more Spiritual Energy overall than we could without your help."

Question: "In other words, we are virtually supplementing the Satellite No. 3 Spiritual Energy release because of the Karmic pattern of mankind, which has a definite implication on the whole Operation?

"Is that correct?"

Answer: "Yes."

Question: "Well, of course, that is very useful information to know and a fact which I have known for some time, **but it is as well for our readers to receive an official reminder from You of this stupendous Truth.**

"If our Spiritual Energy Radiators were not available, then the world would be missing a colossal amount of Spiritual Energy which has been radiated through them.

"Can You verify this for our readers?"

Answer: "That is absolutely correct."

Question: "After such definite verification, I do not think I need the percentage previously requested. I was thinking more about the future; that if we do have an 'ace in the hole,' like, for instance, one or two million Prayer Hours, as we call them, then when Satellite No. 3 is not in orbit, would it be possible, in an emergency situation, to have a broadcast of this Spiritual Energy, even in small amounts, from Central Control?"

Answer: "That would be possible. We will continue communication about this."

Reply: "Well, I think that is absolutely fabulous news!"

Answer: "We must make it clear that such a release would have to be performed under the auspices of Higher Authority and we would have to be informed about it in the correct coded manner."

Question: "We understand and fully accept that!

"Although the Spiritual Energy Radiators are at the service of Satellite No. 3 for 24 hours a day during a Spiritual Push, they would not be of much use unless a beam was put on their receiver coils, would they?"

Answer: "The full answer to that is classified."

Reply: "I know why this answer is classified; one or two more people have been taught this as well."

I was informed that no Spiritual Energy at all, especially during the special runs of the Spiritual Energy Radiators, is wasted; that which has to be absorbed can be kept in 'credit' and such Spiritual Energy can be re-used when necessary.

I was then informed that the Operators of Satellite No. 3 were also thinking about this aspect for the future as well as myself!

I continued with the line of questioning:

Question: "I have been informed by The Cosmic Masters that Satellite No. 3 will operate for at least 2,000 years after The Adepts have left this Planet."

Answer: "That is correct."

Question: "And You are now working out a system where there will be little or no change in the annual operational periods?"

Answer: "Again correct."

Question: "Of course, from our point of view, we would have to pre-book Missions in cooperation with these periods, would we not?"

Answer: "Yes, you would."

Question: "**The Saturn Mission,** for instance, if it continues, and now **Operation Sunbeam** for 16 Phases, have been covered by Satellite No. 3 through our Spiritual Energy Radiators, have they not? These amounted to 213¾ hours of extra running time, releasing 436,050 (four hundred and thirty-six thousand and fifty) Prayer Hours through our Spiritual Energy Radiators."

Answer: "It is not really necessary to **fully cooperate** with Satellite No. 3 during the **Operation Sunbeam** Mission, but imperative during **The Saturn Mission.** That is a definite rule."

Question: "So, in other words, we must plan **The Saturn Mission** during a Spiritual Push, but we could cooperate with the Masters from Gotha to have some Phases of **Operation Sunbeam** performed **outside** of a Spiritual Push on Their request?

"Do I take that as being correct?"

Answer: "Yes, you do. That is a definite statement."

After this, I requested a short break for two reasons, one of which was to ask other people who were present in Santa Barbara at the time, if they had any questions to pose, although I did not tell them any details about the communication which had taken place.

After a short break, I then opened up the communication channel again.

Question: "Thank You for allowing me to continue.

"The only question that seems to crop up, is the amount of Spiritual Energy sent through the original London machine and the ex-**Operation Bluewater** equipment.

"The main coil of the original London machine was made on the suggestion of the Master Aetherius Who did give us some information as to how many coils it should contain and the metal it must be made of, and it did undoubtedly work. The operators always felt a tremendous amount of power through it and it was actually running (naturally, on and off) for 1,650 days, as near as we can judge it.

"Then, as You know, the **Operation Bluewater** equipment was specially made for **Operation Bluewater;** but later, after the Mission, You cooperated with this apparatus from March 15th, 1965 (Earthyear 1.251), and that was running for 598 days.

"We have no idea of how much Spiritual Energy per hour was sent through these machines. However, as both machines were cooperating with the Spiritual Pushes, it would be valuable for us to know, if possible, what amount of Spiritual Energy was involved. (Pause)

"Thank You, You suggest I should rest for a short time now and return to that particular question, and also the other question of 'credit.'

"Well, thank You very much for Your cooperation. Whenever You are ready to open communications again, I am completely at Your service as I have cancelled all other plans at this particular time.

"Thank You for Your consideration."

I took advantage of the short break, which was thoughtfully suggested by the Communicator on Satellite No. 3, and resumed communication again at approximately 11:55 a.m. on May 22nd, 1987 (Earthyear 23.319). I naturally had to re-establish contact with Satellite No. 3 through the coded system and was soon back in communication again.

I still pushed on doggedly with the previous line of questioning, trying to gain whatever information was available while still operating on the ancient occult law — **'it is your questions which will be answered.'**

Question: "To return to the running of these old machines, previous to the activation of the present Spiritual Energy Radiators:

"Now, can You throw any light at all on the amount of Spiritual Energy radiated through them, if You feel that it is worth it? As far as I am concerned, it would be for statistical use only.

"For further explanation, when I talk about total days running, I am talking about the times when these machines were running in conjunction with the orbit of Satellite No. 3.

"Though I realize the equipment was not very good, and also admit that we did have some breakdown time, especially with the London apparatus — and that it was run in poor surroundings in comparison with what the latest machine has now — however, You did state that we are to be duly praised because we did cooperate with Satellite No. 3 in those days, **when there were very few cooperators on Earth** — certainly not in the potent way in which we tried to do it.

"What would be Your most conservative estimate of the total Prayer Hours radiated through these machines, running in London since November 18th, 1959, and the ex-**Operation Bluewater** equipment, running in America since March 15th, 1965 (Earthyear 1.251)?"

Answer: "A most conservative estimation — which is not based on your present figure of 2,040 Prayer Hours discharged each hour which is only applicable to the Spiritual Energy Radiators now in use — **is 2,400,000 (two million, four hundred thousand) Prayer Hours.**

Communication With Satellite No. 3   35

"That is a total for both machines, in all Operations they performed, with the exception of the amount of Spiritual Energy released during **Operation Bluewater,** which is classified.

"Do you understand that correctly?"

Question: "Yes, I do. Thank You very much. That will be good for our overall statistics.

"You realize, do You not, that I did not have long to design and manufacture both of these machines and it is a wonder to me that any Prayer Hours at all could be sent through either of them by Satellite No. 3. However, I take it that Your Controllers took pity on us and You undoubtedly put as many Prayer Hours as You possibly could through what we had to offer.

"Is that correct?"

Answer: "We would not put it in that way. You should be more lenient with yourself and cooperators and admit the fact that we went out of our way to cooperate, with the complete faith that we had in your Operation, which meant a lot to you!"

Question: "Thank You for Your compliments, but I **do** think the figure of 2,400,000 (two million, four hundred thousand) Prayer Hours is a tremendous amount of Healing Energy radiated through machines which I can now only consider to be atrocious-looking pieces of apparatus.

"Was all that used?"

Answer: "Some of it was recalled after operation but eventually it was re-radiated by Satellite No. 3 and all of that Spiritual Energy was used — not at the time it was sent out but later on. **There was no wastage of those Prayer Hours — as you call them — whatsoever."**

Question: "I cannot thank You enough for that.

"Now, to get back to the 'credit' principle, if I may. Again, if our calculations are correct, and they are approximations, can You tell me how many Prayer Hours were actually used from the latest totals? In other words, how much 'credit,' then, as this was mentioned, do we have?

"I see it as a figure which is not really 'cut and dried,' as it were; that some of this Spiritual Energy, although sent through our machines, if not used, **apart from the Missions,** was recalled and then it was later radiated on a sliding scale principle and will possibly continue in this way.

"Could we not, if this Spiritual Energy is stored elsewhere, have some special runs on the Spiritual Energy Radiators **outside** of a Spiritual Push — naturally, of course, with coded information and consent as to when these runs should take place?

"Now I know this may be exceedingly confusing for anyone left in charge, especially when I leave the Planet Earth."

I went on further to state my ideas in this respect and was bold enough (cheeky would be a better word!) to suggest that, as an estimate, if there were say, two million Prayer Hours still not used and had been previously recalled, then this could be put in another place so that, on command by the Custodians, this could be used **outside** of a Spiritual Push, in cases of emergency, if the Satellite was not in orbit.

I was told that this could be possible and if we would like to be given this responsibility, it could be of help to the world as a whole. As I am interested in the world as a whole, I realize that some of the greatest assistance that myself and The Aetherius Society Spiritual Energy Radiator operators can give to man is to use these Spiritual Energy Radiators as much as possible, even when Satellite No. 3 is not in orbit, and I stated that it would be auspicious and helpful if we could do this. I further asked Satellite No. 3 for the amount of Spiritual Energy available in our "Credit Account."

Question: "If, for instance, You have storage Batteries on Central Control, which You have informed me that You do and they are large ones, and I assume there is a Power Radiator available — can they radiate Power strong enough to be picked up by our present Spiritual Energy Radiators without internal modification?"

Answer: "Yes, they can, because They have equipment similar to that we have, only not on such a large scale."

Question: "I know the procedure is going to be very complicated for us but we will make a careful log, to the nearest minute, of all Spiritual Energies which we release and the calculations can be based on 2,040 Prayer Hours discharged per hour of machine run, unless You would like to give us another figure on this 'Credit Energy' release.

"I am sorry to seem so determined about this but I feel it would be of great help to mankind. There may come a time when Satellite No. 3 is uncontactable, and of course, there is no way we can ask You to come into orbit of Earth **outside** Your normal schedule, to help terrestrials. However, I do want to ensure that any Spiritual Energy You 'credit' to us will be put to good use.

"Even if this is only on a temporary measure, it could be done. For instance, the Masters from Gotha are now suggesting further Phases of **Operation Sunbeam.** You have already stated that the Spiritual Energy Radiator coverage for the **Operation Sunbeam** Mission is not essential. But I would respectfully point out that any disaster which may arise during the time You are not in orbit of Terra, may not be fully cared for by our **Operation Prayer Power** Energy. I purposely divorce myself from putting Spiritual Energy into the Prayer Power Batteries because I want to leave **Operation Prayer Power** so that it can be performed by others when I have gone. **That is the true motive behind this line of questioning.**"

Answer: "We will put three million Prayer Hours of Spiritual Energy at your disposal. This Spiritual Energy can be used only on command from Special Advisor S2 and the discharge amount should be worked out at 1,500 Prayer Hours per hour of Spiritual Energy Radiator Operation.

"As time goes on, we will supplement this amount."

Question: "Now You have given me a bomb-blast! This is very generous on Your part!

"May I repeat this to make sure that I received You correctly?

"You said You will put to our 'credit' in Central Control, **three million Prayer Hours** which we have already discharged through the Spiritual Energy Radiators, which was not used and has already been recalled. I understand that this is not the total amount of Spiritual Energy which has been recalled. I do not wish to trouble You with that figure, but for emphasis, we will have a 'credit' of **three million Prayer Hours** and if on command we radiated this, it would be put through either the Spiritual Energy Radiator in London or the one in America, at the rate of 1,500 Prayer Hours per hour of machine operation.

"Is that correct?"

Answer: "Yes."

To help the reader to understand the impact of **three million Prayer Hours:** At the stated rate of discharge, this amount of Spiritual Energy would enable us to run both Spiritual Energy Radiators for three hours a night for three hundred and thirty-three nights continuously. We would not do this, as such discharges would interfere with the Spiritual Pushes. This is merely an illustration to give you the appreciation of the immensity of this much Spiritual Energy.

Question: "I think we are going to have the biggest party we have ever had in the life of The Aetherius Society as a celebration for this!

"You have also just informed me that, as time goes on, You could be even more generous, by a supplementation on this amount?"

Answer: "Yes."

Question: "This will help us very greatly in what we are trying to do for mankind, especially in view of the fact that the next couple of years are going to be, politically, a little awkward, to say the least; but now we have access, in the absence of Satellite No. 3, to this Spiritual Energy, which can be activated on command from Mars Sector 8.

"You know what I am going to ask next, do You not? Well, I

must ask it anyway to be correct in occult Law.

"Supposing I **requested,** for instance, two or three hours run outside of a Spiritual Push. Do You think that request would be turned down or accepted?"

Answer: "I believe the request would be accepted.

"These three million Prayer Hours of Spiritual Energy will be exceptionally potent — **in some ways, even more potent than the Spiritual Energy originally sent through your apparatus.** We are not referring to special emergency runs now; we are talking about the day-to-day Operations."

This statement gave me to understand that these three million Prayer Hours of Spiritual Energy will be so potent, because they have already passed through our machines and thereby have been "humanized," so to speak, by terrestrial contact. The fact that this Spiritual Energy was recalled after it was originally sent out through our apparatus **makes it more potent by Divine and occult Law.**

Further, we have already potentized it by our efforts, in the past, by activating the machines when requested to do so by Higher Authority. This action is counted as an offer to God, by sending out such a stupendous amount of Spiritual Energy on behalf of mankind.

Originally it was sent out.

The Spiritual Energy has not been used.

The Spiritual Energy has been recalled, and the **second** offering we give of the same Spiritual Energy will be more potent than the first offering!

I checked to make sure that this information was correct and on receiving an affirmative answer, replied:

"Sorry I must answer you in typical terrestrial terms: My God! This is fabulous! I do not know how to thank You for this offer."

I was further informed that any radiation of the Spiritual Energy in reserve, must not interfere with any normal Operation of the Spiritual Energy Radiators during a Spiritual Push; neither must it interfere with any special runs of the Spiritual Energy Radiators requested during a Spiritual Push.

Needless to say, I was amazed indeed at this generous offer, and more amazed still when it was stated by the Communicator from Satellite No. 3 that They will try to increase this **three million Prayer Hours bonus,** providing They can do so without over-stepping the Karmic pattern of mankind!

Satellite No. 3 continued:

Answer: "We advise you that this Spiritual Energy should not be used for any personal reasons, with one emergency proviso only."

Question: "I did not visualize it would be used for any personal reasons. However, there is one reason I could envisage here — and I know that I am being extremely forward by this question; however, You realize that I am a soldier from way back!

"However, as certain people in The Aetherius Society have been working exceptionally hard throughout the years, would it be allowable, in Your eyes, Master, if we held a **very** occasional session — and released some of this Spiritual Energy to the most active workers in The Aetherius Society? Could that be counted as a personal reason?"

Answer: "It could not be counted as a purely personal reason and this is allowable. You should work out the ritual to be employed when this is being done; activate a local Spiritual Energy Radiator so that your chosen cooperators may receive some benefit from the Spiritual Energy."

Question: "I was thinking about, possibly say, a few minutes a time? However, You have given me the responsibility of working this out for myself. This, too, is a deep compliment to me. It puts a different light on many, many things.

"Up to now, we have not released **Operation Prayer Power** Energy for the benefit of The Aetherius Society, not even a few minutes of it."

Answer: "There is no Law to stop you from doing so. Your Members put the Prayer Energy into the Battery and are just as much entitled to receive the benefit of it as anybody else on Earth!"

Question: "Then I can work out some ritual which will, shall we say, implement the both types of Spiritual Energy release. I think this would be of great benefit to The Aetherius Society, especially to the Staff Members, most of whom have been active and faithful over the years — as well as some Members?"

Answer: "We suggest, psychologically, it would be auspicious if you occasionally made a short release of Operation Prayer Power Energy to all the people who have participated in Operation Prayer Power." (Note 17.)

Statement: "I agree wholeheartedly with this and am so happy that You agree too, because You know far more about the Law than I do.

"I must apologize, I am now taking a drink of sherry — I need reinforcement after that guidance!

"This is probably the most fantastic conversation I have had since I spoke to The Lords Of The Flame." (Note 18.)

Answer: "You are personally invited to Satellite No. 3 during the next orbit!"

During that statement, the globe of the world on the desk near to me, started to physically shake and when the statement was over, it stopped shaking. I asked:

"Did You make the globe on the desk shake while You were making that statement?"

Answer: "Yes, we did. Not that you need such a demonstration, but we did that."

Statement of Thanks: "No, I did not think the globe was going to fall off the table; however, the perturbations have moved it from its original position. Thank You very much for such a demonstration, especially in view of the statement which was made by You **during** the demonstration.

"This is truly a fabulous conversation!

"I know that people are going to be very interested and very happy about this and I am sure that our **Operation Prayer Power** release to cooperators will help the morale of The Aetherius Society, especially since this is the first time, in all these years, that we have done this. But, I do believe that some people deserve this and I know You believe that, because You suggested it.

"I cannot thank You enough.

"At this time, I cannot think of any further questions I wish to ask and I will be very sorry to see You leave orbit tomorrow because You are deeply revered by all of us. There is a different feeling entirely when You are in orbit.

"When You leave orbit, there is, for me and others — a cold void!

"Although I know we have access to many other great Cosmic Truths, however, this void is still very real."

After making this statement, I shut off the tape and finished off with my personal Blessings to all on Satellite No. 3.

I thanked Them all, with tears of joy in my eyes, for the modern Divine miracle which They had offered to mankind.

I also felt a deep sadness that, although these colossal Spiritual Energies had been given to man, not all of them had been used and some of them had to be recalled.

However, now we were extended the God-given Divine opportunity of using some of the magnificent Spiritual Energy which had hitherto been recalled.

I will never ever forget this — and neither should you, the reader!

The time now in Santa Barbara was just before 12:45 p.m. on May 22nd, 1987 (Earthyear 23.319).

End of present Communique.

COMMUNICATION WITH MARS SECTOR 8 — SPECIAL ADVISOR S2

Almost six hours after the termination of the first communication from Satellite No. 3, I was amazed to receive a further communication, from Mars Sector 8—Special Advisor S2, at 6:35 p.m. on May 22nd, 1987 (Earthyear 23.319), in Santa Barbara. It went like this:

"The three million Prayer Hours — your terminology — has already been transferred to our Battery storage system.

"Sir, you are probably the only person on Terra, and the Realms above, who would have received this bonus.

"We trust you to use it in emergency situations, and as you heard from Satellite No. 3, control must be rested in our hands as to the use of this Spiritual Energy; although, when you feel an emergency situation has arisen, or is arising, you will no doubt inform us of such a situation — on that we have no doubt whatsoever, Sir!

"You are to be congratulated on this action by Satellite No. 3, which was only made because of **Their deference to you and what you have done for all Realms of Terra.**

"Congratulations!"

Question: "Thank You.

"Master, Satellite No. 3 gave me permission to very occasionally make applications to You, when the Satellite is not in orbit, to allow a very limited amount of this Spiritual Energy to be sent to chosen dedicated, faithful Members of The Aetherius Society. I take it that You agree with this?"

Answer: "Most definitely!

"This is Mars Sector 8—Special Advisor S2 ending present communications."

Reply: "This is (Code Name) sending my congratulations and complete support to Mars Sector 8—Special Advisor S2. Thank You for the help which You have given to the Society and myself personally many times in the past, especially that which only Your Sector and myself knows about.

"May the Divine Source of all Creation Bless You for now and all times.

"This is (Code Name) terminating communication with Mars Sector 8—Special Advisor S2."

End of second Communique.

INSIDE THE THIRD SATELLITE

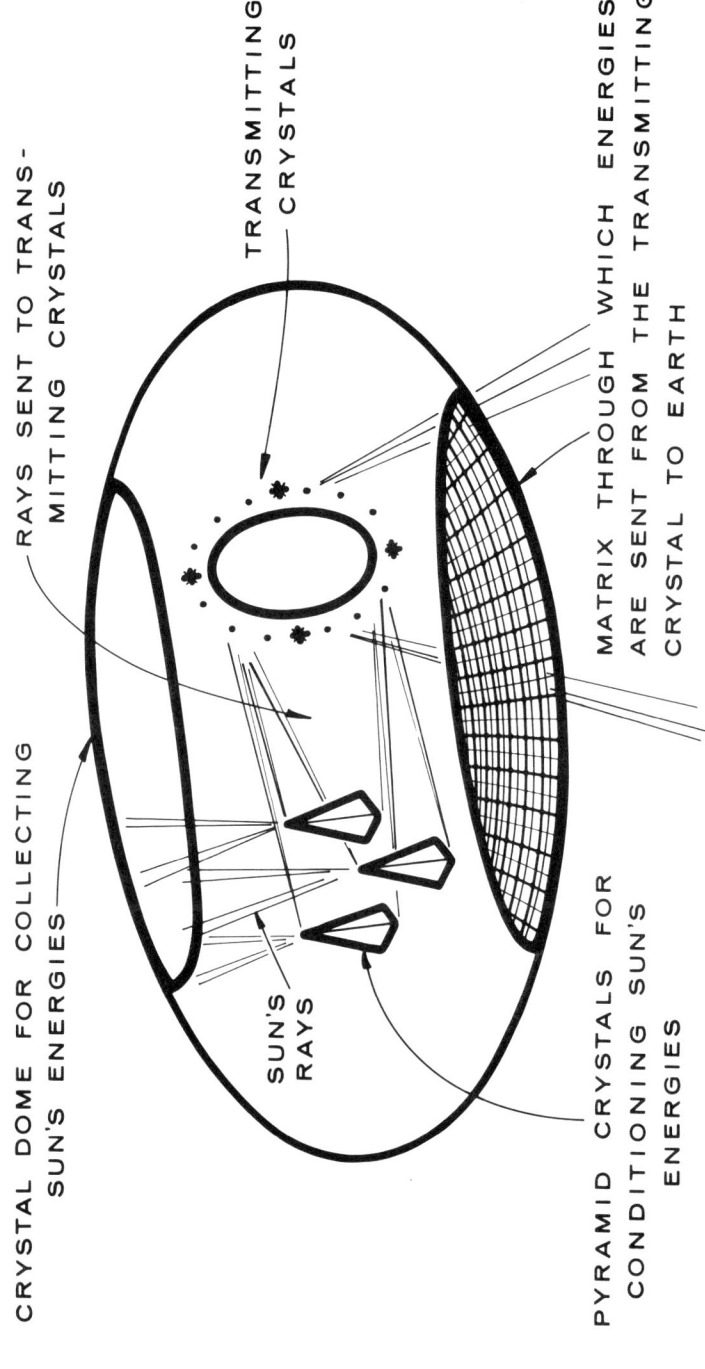

Simplified artist's impression.

©1963 GEORGE KING.

THE SPIRITUAL ENERGY RADIATOR

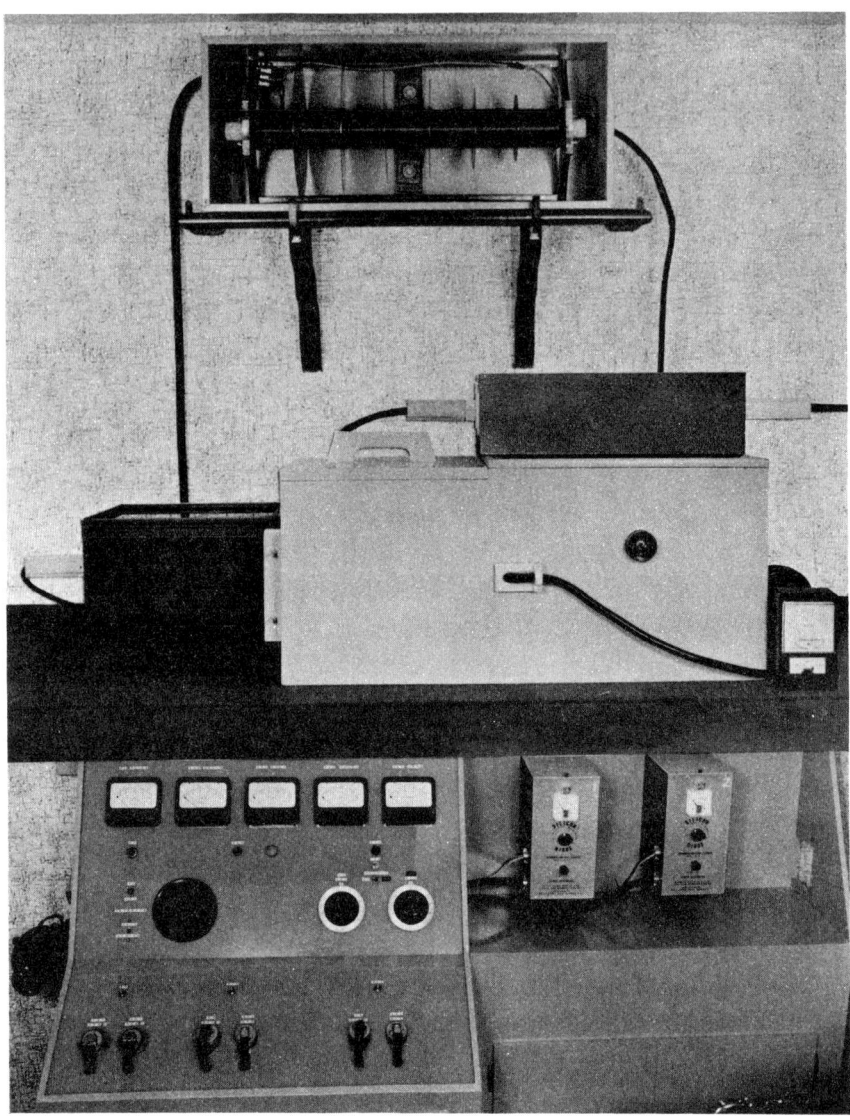

The Spiritual Energy Radiator, designed by the Author and manufactured by the Staff of The Aetherius Society, incorporates advanced concepts of astro-metaphysical science. This remarkable mechanism is one of the two used in **Operation Space Power** in conjunction with Satellite No. 3, both in America and England. Through this apparatus, millions of units of varying frequency Spiritual Energies are transmitted to all Levels of life on Earth. This versatile machine is also used for the release of Prayer Energies in **Operation Prayer Power** discharges.

THE "KING PRANIC CONCENTRATOR"

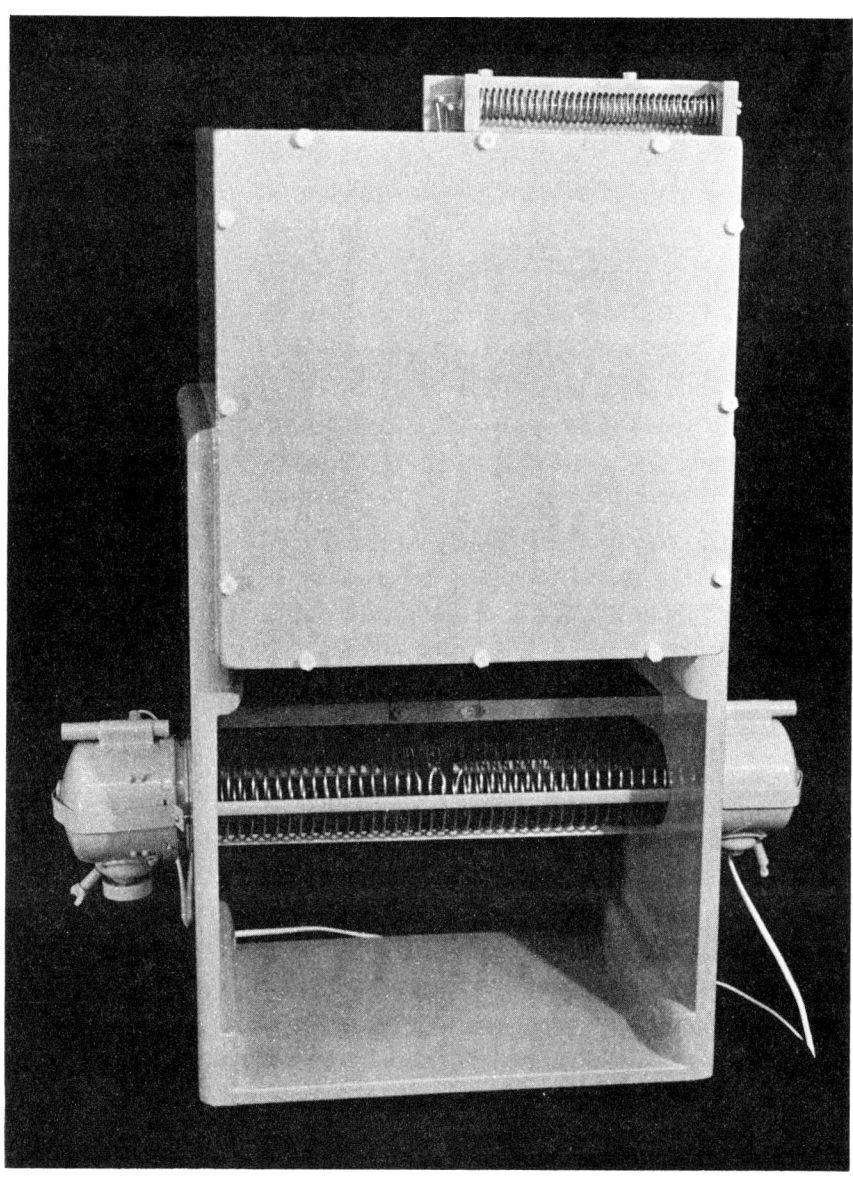

The "King Pranic Concentrator," which was radionically tied in to the rest of the larger equipment in London, from November 18th, 1959, to June 6th, 1971. As stated in the text, this machine ran for 1,650 days in cooperation with Satellite No. 3 during many periods of the Spiritual Push.

OPERATION BLUEWATER APPARATUS

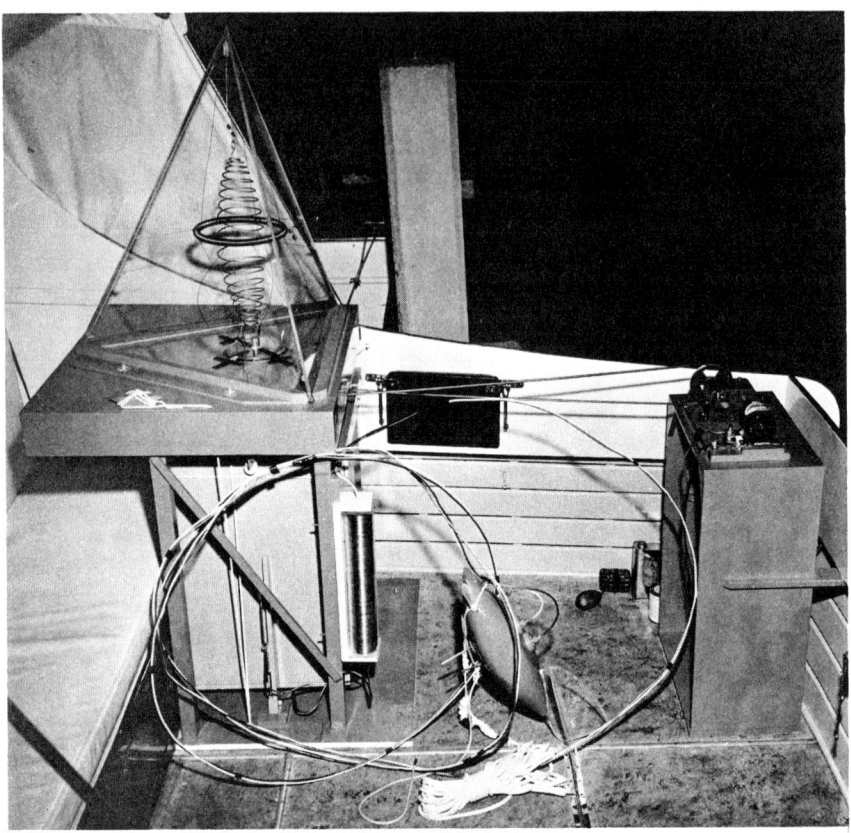

This apparatus, designed by the Author, was used in **Operation Bluewater** to pick up the fluctuating beam of Spiritual Energy from Satellite No. 3. The Spiritual Energy was pulsed, "under pressure," in the main chamber of the machine so that it would travel, through hundreds of feet of sea water, down into a Psychic Centre just off the California coast between Newport Beach and Catalina Island. Although this equipment was originally intended for a few hours use at sea during **Operation Bluewater,** it was subsequently used in almost every Spiritual Push up to October 1969 to radiate Spiritual Energy to mankind in cooperation with Satellite No. 3.

OPERATION BLUEWATER

During the performance of **Operation Bluewater,** the Spiritual Energy picked up by the collector pyramid was conveyed into specially-designed transducers built into the bottom of the float, which was streamed behind the boat. Constant vigilance was necessary to keep the float on an even keel throughout the complex manoeuvres through which the Author had to pilot the boat, so that the transducers would be facing the ocean bottom at all times. It should be noted that the Author not only steered the vessel through these difficult operational patterns, but was, at the same time, tuned into special instructions relayed mentally to him from Satellite No. 3.

OPERATION SUNBEAM — ENGLAND

During **Operation Sunbeam**, the camp site for the Task Force and Mountain Team is meticulously laid out on the side of Holdstone Down, North Devon, England. Nearby, another tent contains the specialized equipment designed by the Author, through which Spiritual Energies are directed, for the benefit of the Planet Terra as an Entity, as a token repayment of the vast Energy debt owed by mankind to this magnificent, compassionate Being. In the foreground is the important CB radio antenna which provides a communications link between the camp and the operations base a few miles away.

OPERATION SUNBEAM — U.S.A.

The **Operation Sunbeam** camp in Padre Bay on Lake Powell, Utah, U.S.A., in late September of 1972. This flooded canyon is surrounded by buttes and plateaus towering hundreds of feet above the desert. Bright sunshine, golden sands, deep red sandstone cliffs and sparkling emerald waters surround the beautiful Psychic Centre of The Mother Earth, the outer perimeter of which is within 300 yards of this camp. The boat is no longer necessary for the performance of the latest improved version of **Operation Sunbeam.**

OPERATION PRAYER POWER

The Mission **Operation Prayer Power** was inaugurated on Holdstone Down, North Devon, England, on June 30th, 1973. In this Mission, Spiritual Energies invoked through the recitation of Holy Mantra are directed towards a select Team skilled in the science of dynamic Prayer, who convey the Energies into a specially-designed Battery capable of holding hundreds of hours of this Prayer Energy. At a later time, this stored Prayer Energy can be released through the Spiritual Energy Radiator and directed to any part of the world to relieve suffering caused by disasters, such as earthquakes, famine or war.

PRAYER POWER DISCHARGE TO ITALY

During **Operation Prayer Power** discharges, the Author acts as Chief Controller and Coordinator throughout the complex manipulations involving cooperation with Higher Forces Who are strategically placed in various parts of the world, indicated on his map. Throughout the discharge, he maintains mental communication with these Cooperators, often controlling several Phases of the Operation which take place simultaneously. In the discharge Operation pictured above, thousands of Prayer Hours of mass Healing Energy were sent to help the injured and the homeless in areas of Italy devastated by an earthquake in November 1980. As well as this, Prayer Energy was also sent to help relief workers in the stricken areas.

PRAYER POWER DISCHARGE TO U.S.A.

In March 1986, Southern California was hit by severe storms and was put on a "tornado watch" after a small tornado struck a densely populated area, causing considerable damage. An **Operation Prayer Power** discharge to the Devic Kingdom brought an immediate improvement in the weather and while the storms continued for a day or so afterwards, the expected tornados did not materialize. In this discharge, Prayer Energy which had previously been taken from an **Operation Prayer Power** Battery in London and was being held by The Adepts, was released directly by Them over the threatened area. As usual, however, the whole Operation was conducted under the control of the Author.

THE SATURN MISSION — SCOTLAND

During the last Sub-Phase of a recent **Saturn Mission** performed in the North of Scotland, the Author, for the first time, brought the boat within a few feet of the end of the jetty built in front of our Scottish base, so that video and still pictures could be taken. This was a very rare occurrence.

THE SATURN MISSION — U.S.A.

In **The Saturn Mission**, devised by The Lords Of Saturn for Devic stabilization and to help the cause of world peace, the Author acts as Chief of Operations on Terra. Here, the Author is seen piloting his boat "Fairseas" from a sheltered cove to the main Operations Centre over a Psychic Centre in America. Everyone who helped in this Mission rejoiced in the fact that, as one result of the successful performance of each Phase — 90,000 people are saved from death or severe mutilation caused by natural catastrophe on Earth.

THE SATURN MISSION — U.S.A.

In the aft cockpit of "Fairseas," a Spiritual Power Battery is securely fastened so that no movement can occur during the delicate manipulations of **The Saturn Mission.** During this Mission, the Author, in constant telepathic communication with the Advanced Intelligence Who acts as Liaison Officer, pilots the boat at slow speed across a Psychic Centre of Earth so that the Spiritual Energies from the Battery can be intermingled with the magnetic interflow of natural Energies radiating from the Psychic Centre.

EPILOGUE

MENTAL COMMUNICATION WITH MARS SECTOR 8—SPECIAL ADVISOR S2, ADEPT ZERO ZERO FIVE AND THE MASTERS FROM GOTHA

This is Santa Barbara; the time is 2:15 p.m.; the date is Thursday, June 18th, 1987 (Earthyear 23.346).

I was here to bring about a mental communication with the Masters from Gotha, Who had, just previous to this, stated Their intention to perform some Phases of **Operation Sunbeam** prior to the next Spiritual Push, which was due to start on July 5th, 1987 (Earthyear 23.363). It was necessary for me to bring about this communication, at the time that I did, because it would probably make a difference to the disposition of Aetherius Society personnel.

We had previously set up an Investiture for "The Mystical Order of Saint Peter" during the afternoon of June 20th (Earthyear 23.348) and this event could not be cancelled because the invitations had been sent out weeks before. (Note 19.)

It was a question of either performing **Operation Sunbeam** from the Headquarters in Los Angeles or from another location available to us in Santa Barbara, California. (For overseas readers, Santa Barbara is 100 miles from Los Angeles.) The Special Missions Task Force Tactical Team would be needed as officials to help run the Investiture, as well as **Operation Sunbeam.** Hence the pressing need to bring about a line of communication with the Gotha Masters involved in a vital part of **Operation Sunbeam.** (Note 20.)

Sometimes it is not too easy to bring about communication with the Three Masters from Gotha Who help in the **Operation Sunbeam** Mission and have done so for many years now.

Epilogue

Question: "This is (Code Name) to the Gotha Masters connected with **Operation Sunbeam**. (Code Name) to Gotha Masters connected with **Operation Sunbeam**. Would You answer me please?"

A few minutes passed and I had not received an answer to my mental communication and, naturally, concluded that there would be some delay.

Therefore, I started further communication with Central Control:

Question: "This is (Code Name) to Mars Sector 8—Special Advisor S2. Please reply Special Advisor S2.

"Special Advisor S2, thank You for being so prompt.

"Let us suppose that the Gotha Masters wished to perform four Phases of **Operation Sunbeam** over the weekend of June 27th and June 28th (Earthyear 23.355/356). Would it be advisable for us to make a special Power Release from our 'Credit Energy' held by Your Sector, during these Phases?"

Answer: "That would be very helpful."

Question: "How many hours, would You estimate, should we run the Spiritual Energy Radiator in Los Angeles?"

Answer: "You should obtain advice on this matter from the Gotha Masters."

Question: "Very well. But would You be willing to make the release when that advice has been given?"

Answer: "We will be willing to make that release whenever the Gotha Masters decide to perform **Operation Sunbeam**."

Question: "Apparently They wanted to perform **Operation Sunbeam** before the start of the next Spiritual Push on July 5th (Earthyear 23.363). Why They wished to do this, I do not know. Could it be because of prevailing world conditions?"

Answer: "That would be the reason."

Question: "Thank You very much; then I will await a reply from Gotha, and may I contact Your Communications Centre later?"

Answer: "Yes, you may."

Reply: "This is (Code Name) temporarily closing down communications with Mars Sector 8—Special Advisor S2."

End of present Communique.

Question: "This is (Code Name) to Nixies Zero Zero Five. If available, please answer me Nixies Zero Zero Five."

The answer came back almost at once and I continued:

"Thank You, Nixies Zero Zero Five.

"I have been trying to communicate with Gotha regarding the next Phases of **Operation Sunbeam** in the near future."

Answer: "I will try to hasten the reply sequence."

Reply: "This is (Code Name) standing by. Thank You very much.

"(Code Name) signing off for now with Nixies Zero Zero Five."

After a wait of approximately two hours, I was mentally contacted again by Adept Zero Zero Five Who stated that the communication was now coming through from the Masters from Gotha.

Question: "This is (Code Name) to Nixies Zero Zero Five.

"You inform me that Gotha are ready to communicate?

"Thank You.

"This is (Code Name) to the Masters from Gotha. Sorry but I do not know You by any other name than that."

Answer: "We extend our greetings and Blessings to all of you."

Reply: "Thank You very much. I will pass that message on to all concerned.

Question: "Now, regarding the next **Operation Sunbeam**

Phases, which I understand You wish to perform before the beginning of the next Magnetization Period which, as You know, will start on July 5th (Earthyear 23.363): I would like to ask You, when would it be really convenient for You to perform these next Phases?"

Answer: "The most convenient time would be, on your calendar, the evenings of June 20th and June 21st (Earthyear 23.348/349). That would be the most auspicious time for us."

Question: "Very well, this can be done.

"Now, are You aware of the previous communications with Satellite No. 3, namely, the holding of **three million Prayer Hours of Spiritual Energy** for us by Mars Sector 8?"

Answer: "We are fully aware of that."

Question: "Now, do You wish to avail Yourself of any coverage during Your **Operation Sunbeam** Phases? I will tell You why I ask the question. If we set up the apparatus over June 20th and 21st (Earthyear 23.348/349), it will be quite easy for us to do this, providing we do so in the Los Angeles Headquarters. Now, if You need coverage, then the Spiritual Energy Radiator will only be a very short distance away from the **Operation Sunbeam** apparatus.

"I was thinking about the possibility of some interference caused by a Spiritual Energy release to the **Operation Sunbeam** apparatus. Other than that, I could leave Los Angeles late on Saturday afternoon, after my Investiture...."

Answer: "That is not necessary. We do not wish to put you to that trouble if it means rushing away from your important Investiture of 'The Mystical Order of Saint Peter.' We would like to perform these Phases from the Temple in Los Angeles."

I had not mentioned the name of the Chivalric Order which was going to hold the Investiture, but in Their answer, the Masters from Gotha proved to me that They, number one, knew this was an important Investiture, and number two, They even gave the name of my Order, namely, "The Mystical Order of

Saint Peter." This shows that They were not ignorant of our main actions.

Question: "Do You wish coverage, because, as You know, I have already communicated with Mars Sector 8—Special Advisor S2 and He has advised me that I had to check with You to see what amount of coverage You desire from the bank of Spiritual Energy held by Central Control."

Answer: "Some coverage would be extremely helpful."

Question: "Are You sure there will not be any interference factor introduced?"

Answer: "Yes."

Reply: "You have already read my mind in this respect, expressing that You feel it would be a good test for the Spiritual Energy coming through our Spiritual Energy Radiator from a source other than Satellite No. 3.

"Well, thank You very much.

"I was rather wanting to do that, and if there will be no interference factor presented by the transmission because of the close proximity of our Spiritual Energy Radiator and the **Operation Sunbeam** apparatus, then it will be better for me to be present on the scene of Operations, rather than 100 miles away from it. I can then take more control and make sure that the Operation goes according to plan."

Answer: "Understandable. We wish to start at 10:00 p.m. Los Angeles time, on June 20th (Earthyear 23.348).

"We will perform two Phases. That will mean a 2:00 a.m. finish.

"On Sunday, June 21st (Earthyear 23.349), we wish to start another two Phases, as usual."

Question: "Very well. Further information can be given to me in private as to the destination, can it not?"

Answer: "Yes."

Question: "We are holding a pilgrimage on July 11th and 12th

Epilogue

(Earthyear 24.4/5) in Commemoration of The Initiation Of Earth and this will be held on Holdstone Down, Devon, England.

"Do You wish to perform more Phases of **Operation Sunbeam** from Holdstone Down, starting on July 11th (Earthyear 24.4)?"

Answer: "We do."

Question: "Thank You very much. So, on the 11th, then, and the 12th, You will hold these Phases from Holdstone Down after the pilgrimage? You see, some people are going down there anyway, so this will present no problem. In fact, the opposite; I have talked to them and they are very keen about it.

"Now, those Phases will be performed during a Spiritual Push and any coverage will come from Satellite No. 3."

Answer: "We agree, thank you."

Question: "What coverage do You require from our apparatus over the weekend of June 20th and 21st (Earthyear 23.348/349)?"

Answer: "We will give these particulars to you prior to our start on June 20th (Earthyear 23.348)."

Reply: "Very well. I have gained all the information necessary at this time and thank You very much for this, and I realize that we must keep up the regular performance of **Operation Sunbeam** because of its vital importance to The Logos Of Earth as a Karmic manipulation."

Answer: "We are all deeply indebted to you and we wish you the very best. I will be in communication with you at a later time to fill in some of the classified details."

Reply: "Thank You very much.

"This is (Code Name) sending his Blessings to the Masters from Gotha Who are helping in **Operation Sunbeam**. May You be Blessed."

Answer: "We also send our Blessings to you and all cooperators in **Operation Sunbeam**."

Reply: "Thank You. That is very nice of You.

"This is (Code Name) terminating communication, for this time, with the Masters from Gotha."

Answer: "We are terminating communications with the Blessings on your heads from the Divine Source of all Creation."

Reply: "Thank You very much indeed. This is a great honour which we deeply appreciate."

End of Communique.

THE START OF OPERATION SPACE POWER II

The Investiture, starting at 2:30 p.m. on Saturday, June 20th (Earthyear 23.348), went off very well indeed. Several nice people who had been engaged, for many years, in different charity works, were dubbed into "The Mystical Order of Saint Peter," which is an Ecumenical Order of Chivalry and one which is highly respected by prominent figures in nobility throughout the world.

However, the garden party following had to be closed down just after 5:00 p.m. so that preparations could be made to set up the **Operation Sunbeam** equipment in our Temple.

Between the hours of 10:00 p.m. and 2:00 a.m. on Saturday and Sunday, June 20th/21st (Earthyear 23.348/349), two Phases of **Operation Sunbeam** were successfully performed.

The Spiritual Energy Radiator was run, on the request of the Masters from Gotha, from 12 midnight to 2:00 a.m. June 21st (Earthyear 23.349), which lent a powerful coverage and Energy boost to the Operation itself.

The Masters from Gotha transmitted through the Operation Sunbeam apparatus, directly tuned into a Psychic Centre of Earth, 6,000 Prayer Hours of very high frequency Spiritual Energy during these two Phases, Phase 249 and Phase 250.

At the same time, we released 3,000 Prayer Hours (at the rate of 1,500 Prayer Hours per hour of Spiritual Energy Radiator Operation: see text) from the "Energy Credit" which was being held for our further use. It has been decided that this aspect of the Mission is called **Operation Space Power II.** (Note 21.)

On June 21st/22nd (Earthyear 23.349/350), two more Phases of Operation Sunbeam were performed, Phase 251 and Phase 252, and a further 6,000 Prayer Hours of Spiritual Energy were transmitted through our Operation Sunbeam apparatus, by the Masters from Gotha, to The Logos Of Earth.

At the Masters' request, we ran the Spiritual Energy Radiator for another two hours, from 12 midnight to 2:00 a.m. June 22nd (Earthyear 23.350), and even another 3,000 Prayer Hours were transmitted through this machine.

This made a total of 12,000 Prayer Hours released to The Logos Of Earth by the Masters from Gotha, and **6,000 Prayer Hours released through our Spiritual Energy Radiator,** which were manipulated by the Masters from Gotha to a classified destination, for the benefit of all mankind!

The totals in the statistical section of this book do not include the Spiritual Energy released in **Operation Sunbeam** in the beginning when the Spiritual Energy Radiators were used, as this section deals mainly with Spiritual Energy transmitted through our Spiritual Energy Radiators in **Operation Space Power.** The **Operation Sunbeam** releases are kept separately.

Certain of us in The Aetherius Society have worked long and diligently in order to gain the honoured position which we now hold, namely, that of being the custodians for a tremendous amount of Spiritual Energy; and the Author, as per statements made in the text, is completely trusted by The Cosmic Masters to use this glorious, uplifting, Healing Power in the right way. This, in itself, is one of the greatest compliments ever paid to anyone!

And thus we go on, Operation after Operation, Spiritual Push after Spiritual Push, releasing Spiritual Energy to the world which, had we not had the Spiritual Energy Radiators available, and had we lacked dedication, this uplifting, Healing Power could not have been sent to mankind — or to you!

This is the gist of the statements made by the Masters Themselves, and not only we of The Aetherius Society.

Whether the reader agrees with this statement or not, does not alter the fact that it is true.

It is also true that The Aetherius Society is the only organization, on the physical planes of Earth, which has been given such an enormous trust as this.

We are not a huge organization and definitely not a very rich one; but all the physical plane influence and physical plane money cannot buy units of Spiritual Energy from Satellite No. 3.

This commodity is not for sale!

It has taken us years of work, under the all-seeing Eye of the Great Masters from Satellite No. 3, to bring about the true facts you can read in this book.

If you also, **as you all should,** study the Author's Recommendations, you will see open before you, an extensive new study course on many aspects of Cosmic Wisdom which are happening today on this Earth.

Those who see this must be led by their own conscience to give us the loyalty, help and support which we need in order to continue these greatest of all tasks on Earth today, namely, **Operation Space Power, Operation Sunbeam, The Saturn Mission** and **Operation Prayer Power.**

Each of these Missions has an Essence of God the Overall Creator, shining through it like an all-pervasive, all-illuminating Light of true Service to humanity.

And thus we continue to serve humanity, in the past — in the present — and into the future.

May God Bless you all.

OPERATION SPACE POWER

SPIRITUAL ENERGY RADIATOR ACTIVATION IN CONJUNCTION WITH SATELLITE NO. 3

May 28th, 1955 to May 23rd, 1987

London original machine and "King Pranic Concentrator":
    Started cooperation: November 18th, 1959
    Ended cooperation: June 6th, 1971

Total days running in conjunction with Satellite No. 3: 1,650 days

Los Angeles Operation Bluewater equipment:
    Started cooperation: March 15th, 1965
    Ended cooperation: October 9th, 1969

Total days running in conjunction with Satellite No. 3: 598 days

Total days running between London and Los Angeles: 2,248 days

Total Spiritual Energy released through the London machine and the Operation Bluewater machine running in conjunction with Satellite No. 3: 2,400,000 Prayer Hours*

Special Note: This information was given directly from Satellite No. 3 to the Author on May 22nd, 1987.

OPERATION SPACE POWER

SPIRITUAL ENERGY RADIATOR ACTIVATION IN CONJUNCTION WITH SATELLITE NO. 3

May 28th, 1955 to May 23rd, 1987
(This Mission is still continuing)

Current Spiritual Energy Radiators

Los Angeles Spiritual Energy Radiator — started cooperation:	March 1st, 1969
Hours run in Operation Space Power in conjunction with Satellite No. 3:	7,155¾ hours
Operation Space Power Prayer Hours transmitted to date: (by calculation)	14,597,730 Prayer Hours (approximately)
London Spiritual Energy Radiator — started cooperation:	June 7th, 1971
Hours run in Operation Space Power in conjunction with Satellite No. 3:	6,120 hours
Operation Space Power Prayer Hours transmitted to date: (by calculation)	12,484,800 Prayer Hours (approximately)
Total Operation Space Power Prayer Hours transmitted through the Los Angeles and London current machines to May 23rd, 1987:	**27,082,530 Prayer Hours** or **3,091.6 Prayer Years** (approximately)

OPERATION SPACE POWER

SPIRITUAL ENERGY RADIATOR ACTIVATION IN CONJUNCTION WITH THE CURRENT SPIRITUAL MISSIONS OF THE AETHERIUS SOCIETY

June 30th, 1973 to May 23rd, 1987
(These Missions are still continuing)

Operation Sunbeam

Total hours run: 65 hours
(1986 and 1987 only)

Total Prayer Hours transmitted: 132,600 Prayer Hours

The Saturn Mission

Total hours run: 148¾ hours
(1986 and 1987 only)

Total Prayer Hours transmitted: 303,450 Prayer Hours

Combined total of Prayer Hours released through the Spiritual Energy Radiators in conjunction with Operation Sunbeam and The Saturn Mission:

Total Hours run: 213¾ hours
Total Prayer Hours transmitted: 436,050 Prayer Hours

The actual amount of Spiritual Energy released to the Devic Kingdom during The Saturn Mission is strictly classified information.

OPERATION PRAYER POWER

June 30th, 1973 to May 23rd, 1987

Summation of Spiritual Energy released through the current Spiritual Energy Radiators in Los Angeles and London — direct from Spiritual Power Batteries:

Total Prayer Hours discharged: 95,955 Prayer Hours or
10.95 Prayer Years

SUMMATION OF THE OPERATIONS OF SATELLITE NO. 3

May 28th, 1955 to May 23rd, 1987

(These figures are for the first 32 years of cooperation. These Missions are still continuing.)

Number of days Satellite No. 3 was in Magnetization Orbit of Terra: **4,171 days**

Spiritual Energy sent directly from Satellite No. 3 to mankind upon Terra:

   To Life Levels 5 and 6: **Between 54,223,000,000 and 72,992,500,000 Units of Spiritual Energy**

Special Note: This Spiritual Energy is not classifiable under the normal "Prayer Hour" classification.

   To Life Levels +4 through −4: **Between 130,656,575 and 194,577,150 Prayer Hours of Spiritual Energy**

Spiritual Energy sent from Satellite No. 3 through the original London radionic machine and "King Pranic Concentrator" and the Operation Bluewater machine in Los Angeles:

2,400,000 Prayer Hours

Special Note: This **excludes** the total amount of Spiritual Energy radiated during the actual Operation Bluewater itself. This amount is strictly classified information.

SUMMATION OF THE OPERATIONS OF SATELLITE NO. 3

May 28th, 1955 to May 23rd, 1987
(Continued)

Spiritual Energy sent through the current Spiritual Energy Radiators in Los Angeles and London in conjunction with Operation Sunbeam and The Saturn Mission:

436,050 Prayer Hours

Spiritual Energy sent through the current Spiritual Energy Radiators in Los Angeles and London (**including** that sent in conjunction with Operation Sunbeam and The Saturn Mission):

27,082,530 Prayer Hours

Spiritual Energy sent out to the world from Operation Prayer Power:

95,955 Prayer Hours

SPECIAL NOTE RE OPERATION SUNBEAM:

Total estimated Spiritual Energy sent through the Operation Sunbeam apparatus direct to The Logos Of Earth:

661,000 Prayer Hours

GRAND TOTALS OF SPIRITUAL ENERGY RELEASED DURING COOPERATION WITH SATELLITE NO. 3

May 28th, 1955 to May 23rd, 1987

Spiritual Energy sent to Levels 5 and 6:
- Minimum: **54,223,000,000 Units**
- Maximum: **72,992,500,000 Units**

Spiritual Energy sent to Levels +4 to −4:
- Minimum: **130,656,575 Prayer Hours**
- Maximum: **194,577,150 Prayer Hours**

Total Spiritual Energy released through the original London and Los Angeles machines: **2,400,000 Prayer Hours**

Total Spiritual Energy released through the current London and Los Angeles machines, including Operation Space Power and cooperation during Operation Sunbeam and The Saturn Mission: **27,082,530 Prayer Hours**

Total Spiritual Energy released through Operation Prayer Power: **95,955 Prayer Hours**

GRAND TOTAL of Spiritual Energy released through original and current machines: **29,578,485 Prayer Hours** or **3,376.5 Prayer Years**

AUTHOR'S RECOMMENDATIONS

AN OUTLINE OF AN ADVANCED STUDY COURSE ON THE TEXT

NOTE 1.   The Transmission from the Master Aetherius containing information about the actions of Satellite No. 3, is published in *Cosmic Voice, Volume 1.*

NOTE 2.   For information on the Operation of Satellite No. 3, study Chapter 4 of *The Nine Freedoms; The Day The Gods Came; Operation Sunbeam — God's Magic In Action;* and *Cosmic Voice, Volume 1,* pages 32 - 35 and 73 - 79.

NOTE 3.   If a large volume of Spiritual Energy is sent to any place on the surface of the Planet Earth and this Spiritual Energy is used in unselfish ways, to help others, for mass healing, etc., then what we call a "resonance factor" does not build up. If, however, on the other hand, an amount of this Spiritual Energy is **not** used by the people who then populate the Spiritualized area, there is a build up of what we term a "resonance factor." This "resonance factor" has to be balanced at once by the recall of the surplus, unused Spiritual Energies. This balance has been brought about several times in the past by both The Cosmic Masters and The Adepts.

NOTE 4.   **Operation Bluewater** was a complex metaphysical Operation performed in 1963 and 1964 off the coast of California, U.S.A. The successful completion of this Operation prevented a major earthquake and resultant tidal wave which would have devastated a large part of the western American coastline. **Operation Bluewater** was assigned to the Author by The Cosmic Masters and involved the transmission of immense Spiritual Energies to the Planet Earth as an Entity.

For details of this Cosmic Mission, read the booklet, *This Is The Hour Of Truth;* Chapter 4 of *The Five Temples Of God;* and *The Aetherius Society Newsletter,* Volumes 2, 3 and 4, 1963 - 1965.

NOTE 5. **Operation Sunbeam** is a Cosmic Mission originally designed by the Author and performed by The Aetherius Society, and mainly by the Masters from Gotha, in which Spiritual Energies, originally intended for the use of mankind, are directed through specialized equipment into certain Psychic Centres of Earth as a token repayment of the vast energy debt owed by mankind to The Logos Of Earth. Because of the vast Karmic implications of **Operation Sunbeam,** it has been declared by Cosmic Sources to be an integral part of the Cosmic Plan for world salvation and enlightenment.

Further understanding of this Mission can be gained by a study of the following Aetherius Society publications: Cassette No. C-54, *Operation Sunbeam;* Metacassette® No. MC-2, *Operation Sunbeam Inspires The Galaxy;* and Metacassette® No. MC-19, *Gotha Speaks To Earth.* Also read, *Operation Sunbeam — God's Magic In Action* and *Eternal Recognition of Operation Sunbeam.*

The history of this Mission has also been recorded in *The Aetherius Society Newsletter* and Journal *Cosmic Voice.* Details are obtainable from the publishers, The Aetherius Society.

NOTE 6. On June 14th, 1979, after months of intensive research and design of new equipment, the Author introduced an improved modus operandi in **Operation Sunbeam,** which greatly potentized the Mission by enabling double the amount of Spiritual Energy to be released to The Logos Of Earth during each Phase, while at the same time, considerably increasing the number of Phases which could be performed in any year. For further information, read *The Aetherius Society Newsletter,* Volume 18, Issues 19-22,

October 1979; Issues 29-32, November/December 1979; and Volume 19, Issues 11-14, June/July 1980.

NOTE 7.   **Operation Prayer Power,** a Cosmic Mission designed by the Author, is the most potent terrestrial mass healing tool ever devised for the use and benefit of ordinary man. In this Mission, Prayer Energy invoked by dedicated people is stored in Spiritual Energy Batteries, which can be released, at any time, through the Spiritual Energy Radiators and directed to any part of the world to alleviate suffering in times of disaster.

For a greater understanding of this Mission, study of the following cassettes is recommended: Cassette No. C-52, *Operation Prayer Power;* Metacassette® No. MC-12, *Operation Prayer Power — A Spiritual Dream Come True;* Metacassette® No. MC-13, *Important Declaration Of Truth To Terra;* and Metacassette® No. MC-21, *The Inauguration of Operation Prayer Power On Level Four.*

The history of this Mission has also been recorded in *The Aetherius Society Newsletter* and Journal *Cosmic Voice.* Details are obtainable from the publishers, The Aetherius Society.

For information on how to participate in this on-going Mission, contact your nearest Headquarters of The Aetherius Society and read the pamphlet, *Operation Prayer Power — A Spiritual Dream Come True,* obtainable free of charge.

NOTE 8.   In a Transmission delivered by the Cosmic Master Mars Sector 8 through the Author on November 17th, 1977, it was stated that, starting with the Magnetization Periods of 1978, Satellite No. 3 would cooperate with the Mission **Operation Prayer Power** by manipulating Prayer Energy released from the Prayer Power Batteries throughout each Spiritual Push. See *The Aetherius Society Newsletter,* Volume 17, Issues 1-4, January/February 1978.

Since that time, regular discharges of Prayer Energy

from the **Operation Prayer Power** Batteries have been made on specific days each week during every Spiritual Push, to be manipulated by Satellite No. 3 for the benefit of the world as a whole.

NOTE 9.   Read *Operation Sunbeam — God's Magic In Action* for further information regarding the categories of Spiritual Energy.

NOTE 10. Study of the following material by the Author, a world-renowned expert on the Law of Karma, is recommended: *Karma And Reincarnation* (this small booklet contains one of the most concise and straightforward explanations of Karma obtainable); Chapter 9 of *The Twelve Blessings,* as delivered through the Author by The Master Jesus; *The Nine Freedoms; You Are Responsible!; The Day The Gods Came; The Three Saviours Are Here!; The Five Temples Of God; Operation Sunbeam — God's Magic In Action.*

Also, listen to the following cassettes: Cassette No. C-14, *The Spiritual Energy Crisis;* Cassette No. C-15, *Karma And Reincarnation;* Cassette No. C-20, *The Cosmic Plan;* and Cassette No. C-31, *If I Could Choose.*

The following Transmissions from Cosmic Sources, delivered through the Author, contain invaluable Wisdom on the Law of Karma and are available on cassettes: Metacassette® No. MC-14, *Ye Are Gods;* Metacassette® No. MC-15, *From Freewill To Freedom;* Metacassette® No. MC-16, *Action Is Essential;* and Metacassette® No. MC-17, *Fight Ye The Evil.*

NOTE 11. **The Saturn Mission,** which started in Scotland in September 1981, is a special Operation devised by The Lords Of Saturn Who assigned the Author to be Their Chief of Operations on Terra. During this Mission, Spiritual Energies are released over a Psychic Centre of Earth to intermingle with the natural Energies radiating from that Psychic Centre, and are sent to the Devic

Kingdom so that they will help to bring about a stabilization of natural conditions on Earth. The full results of **The Saturn Mission** are unknown; however, one of the massive side results of this Mission is that for every complete Phase performed, at least 90,000 people are saved from death or severe mutilation caused by natural catastrophe.

The history of this Mission, together with evidence of its miraculous results, has been recorded in the Journal *Cosmic Voice.* Details are obtainable from the publishers, The Aetherius Society.

NOTE 12. For details of the special Operations on the Spiritual Energy Radiators in conjunction with **The Saturn Mission,** read *Cosmic Voice,* Volume 7, Issues 8-9, July; Issues 10-11, August/September; Issues 12-14, October/December 1986; and Volume 8, Issues 2-6, March/April 1987.

NOTE 13. The Cosmic Master Mars Sector 8—Special Advisor S2, in two mental communications with the Author, supplied information enabling far greater precision in the calculation of Spiritual Energy within the **Operation Prayer Power** Batteries. See *The Aetherius Society Newsletter,* Volume 17, Issue 19, August 1978; and Volume 18, Issues 23-24, October 1979.

NOTE 14. This "resonance factor" has been evident during several **Operation Prayer Power** discharges. These include the discharge to Italy on November 24th, 1980, following an earthquake there; the discharge of April 23rd, 1981, for the benefit of Poland; and the discharge on September 21st, 1985, to Mexico following the devastating earthquake in that country. For further details, read *Cosmic Voice,* Volume 1, Issues 5-8, October/November 1980; Volume 2, Issues 10-12, August/September 1981; and Volume 7, Issues 4-7, April/June 1986.

NOTE 15. For details on some of the miraculous results of the **Operation Prayer Power** discharges in emergency situations, read *The Aetherius Society Newsletter,* Volume 12,

Issues 16-20, August/September; and Issues 25-26, December 1974; and *Cosmic Voice,* Volume 1, Issues 5-8, October/November 1980; Volume 4, Issues 1-4, January/March 1983; Volume 6, Issues 1-4, January/March 1985; and Volume 7, Issues 4-7, April/June 1986.

NOTE 16. For further information regarding the planes of existence, listen to Cassette No. C-11, *Levels of Consciousness, Part 1 — 'The Spirit World';* Cassette No. C-12, *Levels of Consciousness, Part 2 — 'Realms Of The Masters';* and Cassette No. C-68, *Life After Death.*

Also read *The Three Saviours Are Here* regarding life on the lower levels of existence, referred to as the "hells," published by The Aetherius Society. This information is unobtainable from any other source.

NOTE 17. **Special Note:** This statement, made by the Cosmic Master from Satellite No. 3, will undoubtedly bring great joy to the hearts of many of our Members. However, it must be pointed out that The Aetherius Society has Members in many different parts of the world outside of Britain and the United States, such as Australia, New Zealand, Nigeria, Ghana, etc. These Members, because of their geographical position, have not had a chance to participate in **Operation Prayer Power,** but they will not be victimized because of this.

Many attenders throughout Nigeria and New Zealand have been practising the Mantra and Prayers very diligently for a considerable time now, so even though these Members have not actually participated in front of a Prayer Power Battery, they have shown their willingness to do so by their regular practise. The regular attenders to these Branch practice sessions will be included in the overall ritual when, as the Master suggests, a Prayer Power Energy release from the Batteries is made to Members who have participated.

It is worth noting that, now The Aetherius Society is

registered by the Federal Government of Nigeria as a Church, it will be possible for us to send over a remote module so that they can physically participate in **Operation Prayer Power,** and we will work in order to bring this about.

Therefore, as stated, our remote Members will not be forgotten.

NOTE 18. For further information about the **Three Ancient Lords Of The Flame,** Who have accepted the responsibility as Protectors of The Life Force of The Logos of this Planet, read the book, *Visit To The Logos Of Earth.* This is a true story which describes, in graphic detail, the supernormal experiences of the Author, who made two visits deep into the centre of Earth, near the living Heart of the Planet. This is classed as one of the finest books ever written about this subject and is published with the full knowledge and Blessings of The Lords Of The Flame, thereby making the book a truly remarkable and Holy work.

NOTE 19. "The Mystical Order of Saint Peter" is an Ecumenical Order of Chivalry, founded in England in 1981 and incorporated in the United States of America as a Religious, non-profit making, charitable organization. Any further information regarding this Order may be obtained from the publishers of this book.

NOTE 20. Listen to Cassette No. C-72, *A Physical Space Contact With A Master From Gotha* and Metacassette® No. MC-19, *Gotha Speaks To Earth,* which contain valuable Spiritual lessons and explain the presence on Earth of advanced Intelligences from the System of Gotha in order to help in **Operation Sunbeam.** These Masters, originally two and later joined by a third, play a vital role in the Mission by transmitting high frequency Spiritual Energy through The Aetherius Society apparatus to The Logos Of Earth.

NOTE 21. The name **Operation Space Power II** is given to a release through our Spiritual Energy Radiators of portions of the three million units of "Credit Energy" so kindly allocated to us by Satellite No. 3. We have given the Mission this name so that there can be no confusion in the minds of our readers when they study statistics of releases made during the main **Operation Space Power.**

Operation Space Power is the name given to a Cosmic Mission relating to Spiritual Energy sent directly from Satellite No. 3 through our Spiritual Energy Radiators.

Operation Space Power II is the name of a Cosmic Mission where Spiritual Energy is transmitted from Central Control, Mars Sector 8—Special Advisor S2, with Their sanction, from the "Credit Energy" They are holding for our use.

The first use of the "Credit Energy" was on June 21st and 22nd, 1987, in conjunction with **Operation Sunbeam,** when the following Phase of **Operation Space Power II** was performed through our Spiritual Energy Radiator in the United States:

Total Spiritual Energy Radiator hours run:	4 hours
Total Prayer Hours transmitted:	6,000 Prayer Hours
Total Prayer Hours remaining in "Credit Energy" bank:	2,994,000 Prayer Hours